14

THE FLIES IN MY HAT

The Flies in my Hat

A book about Trout Fishing in New Zealand

by

GREG KELLY

HODDER AND STOUGHTON

First published 1967
Second impression 1968

SBN: 340 02688 X

Printed in Great Britain for Hodder and
Stoughton Limited, St. Paul's House,
Warwick Lane, London, E.C.4, by Cox
and Wyman Limited, London, Fakenham
and Reading

To Truda, who for twenty years has shared a sympathetic understanding of angling and anglers and who has helped me greatly in many ways to prepare the manuscript of this book.

Acknowledgements

I should like to express my thanks to many friendly fishermen who have come so readily to my assistance with their cameras.

The illustrations used in this book have been credited to the photographer in every possible case, but I feel that I must mention in particular the Venerable Archdeacon Young (Riwaka), Denis Shuker (Motueka), Bryan Atkinson and Jeff Hamilton (Taupo), Des Hayes and Les Mark (Taumarunui), and Arthur Hamilton (Invercargill), who all made special journeys, sometimes more than one, to favourite angling reaches on my behalf.

I much appreciate the courtesy of the *Weekly News*, The Tourist and Publicity Department and the *Taupo Times* for their permission to use official photographs.

I am grateful to my frank trout-stalking accomplice Ted Webber of Havelock North for his lively Introduction — which nearly sent me spinning! — and to my companion to Whakapapa, Peter McIntyre, for the painting of my battered old fishing hat to which the magic of his brush has lent an air of respectability.

I sincerely appreciate the kindness of Neil Robinson of Auckland, who was the first to read the manuscript, in introducing it and the writer to the House of Hodder and Stoughton Ltd.

G. G. K.
Taupo

Introduction

Though I have argued, in the past, that an introduction to a book may be like an introduction to people at a cocktail party – in that it often may not register and may therefore be held to be unnecessary – there are admitted exceptions. One of them is the introduction to a book about trout fishing.

There are those who are interested in fishing for trout – which in New Zealand today is much too large a section of the community – who like to know something about the background and qualifications of those who set themselves up to write for their edification.

They like to know either that the man is an admitted mug, who is simply trying to compensate for his lack of knowledge by trying to be funny about fishing, or that he is a man of experience, judgement and skill who is prepared to share these qualifications with his readers. I fall into the first category myself; my old friend Greg Kelly falls into the second.

It is therefore a great gratification to me to be invited to write an introduction to *The Flies In My Hat*. I have felt for a long time that Greg Kelly should write a book about his sixty years of fishing – he caught his first trout in 1907 – and I have urged him to write such a book. He has already written one book about his lifetime experience with firearms (*The Gun In The Case*, published in 1963), and it is only fitting he should make it plain that he had devoted just as much time to angling as he had done to shooting and ballistics. He has also, of course, devoted a lot of time to earning a living, but that is immaterial, though a tribute to Kelly's ingenuity.

As this book will demonstrate, there are very few parts of New Zealand in which Greg Kelly has not fished, but he has done much more than that. Greg knows, better than most, that the really happy and successful angler is the man who is not only a student of trout in their lurking places, but of the enthralling world of nature around every river bank and lake shore.

Greg is not only an extremely knowledgeable angler; he is also extremely knowledgeable about birds, trees, insects, animals and his fellow men – particularly his fellow fishermen. All this emerges in the book. There is a lot more inside, or under, the Kelly hat than trout flies – though I have observed, nevertheless, that this interesting specimen of composted headgear carries some very choice specimens of the latter.

Admittedly there are no established qualifications for writing a book about trout fishing and consequently some very odd people pursue this pastime. But Greg Kelly *has* qualifications. He served for thirteen years as a member of the council of the Auckland Acclimatisation Society and for almost as long as a councillor of the Waimarino Society. Then, combining business with pleasure, he managed a sporting goods firm in Auckland and another in Rotorua, and he has also had many years' experience as an honorary ranger.

It is this ranging experience, possibly, that has given Kelly a slightly magisterial look. He has it when he watches a mug caster – of whom he knows a number – and he doubtless had it when he emerged with his well-known bushcraft from the undergrowth to accost some hapless dappler with huhu grubs operating on good fly water.

But it is not my purpose to anticipate the Kelly reminiscences as they appear in the following pages.

Greg Kelly, as I can testify, is that rare and valuable character, an angler who values the sport above the results, who is content with the river as he finds it and his companionship as he meets it. Angling in New Zealand, as in older countries where it evolved, owes a debt to its wise men, and among these I number Greg Kelly. I am glad, therefore, that at the age of seventy-nine he has at last put some of his fishing philosophy and some of his angling experiences on record.

Havelock North   E. G. Webber

Contents

Illustrations

CREDITS TO ILLUSTRATIONS

National Publicity Studios, New
    Zealand. [1, 4, 5, 10]
Denis Shuker. [2]
A. H. Hamilton [3]
Ted Webber. [6, 7]
K. Draper. [8, 9]

J. Siers. [11]
Taupo Times [13, 14]
Des Hayes. [15]
Les Mark. [16, 18]
New Zealand Weekly News. [19]
L. B. Atkinson. [21]

Lake Taupo. A fisherman plays his fish as he manoeuvres it to the beach at the Waitahanui River

Riwaka River, Nelson Province

Otapiri River in Southland

1. The Flies in my Hat

This morning, in clear, bright sunshine, I watched an elderly angler on the beach at Taupo playing a fish.

The fish broke the surface in high, flashing leaps, each one closer to the shore. The angler was in no hurry, being quite content to keep a steady tension on the line as he followed the course of the fighting trout along the beach. Plainly this man had handled trout before, probably thousands of them.

After eleven minutes' struggle the fish was splashing in the shallows in its last desperate efforts to get free; but to no purpose. It was then that the angler nearly lost. As he stooped stiffly down to toss the trout out on the sand, his aged body failed to bend far enough, and his hand slipped off its mark. Violent splashing followed, but the hook held, and in his next attempt, the ancient one managed to get his hand under the fish and throw it out. After killing his fish the old man held it up to look at it. It was easy to imagine the glint in his eye and the smile on his face. His bright rainbow would have weighed at least three pounds.

The angler was unknown to me. I should have liked to leave the car and ask him the usual questions one angler asks another: "What did you take him on?"; but left him alone to enjoy his wonderful moment in peace.

He wore a cap and I'm sure he carried no spare or rejected fly in it. Did he simply use one fly, or did he have his spares stuck in the lapels of his coat? I wish now that I had asked him, for I am sure he would have understood. He would know that behind the question stands the bulk of angling knowledge — the fly for the particular water, the fly for that day and season, or the fly for which the fish are rising.

As I look at my old tweed hat I am reminded of my failures and triumphs. There's hardly a fly there that is not of a famous pattern. Picking it up recently, my wife made an intriguing remark; "Kelly, those dry flies are all in a huddle of their own. They look like a bunch of little snobs."

Certainly they did look exclusive and superior. "Why not?" I thought. Most of them are of long lineage from the most exclusive waters in the world, the chalk streams of Hampshire. Their patterns were developed by the great dry-fly masters such as Halford, Hardy, Hofland, Dewar and Hills. They were used by Mottram, Skues, Viscount Grey, Charles Kingsley and Senior, who brought his "small floating flies" to fish the Cust in Canterbury five years after brown trout were first liberated there.

My "little snobs" have given me absorbing excitement on the sparkling, babbling rivers of Mid-Canterbury, Nelson, Southland and the West Coast. Given the right water and the essential time they hold the same promise of pleasure now as they gave their designers in England, Wales, Cornwall, Scotland and Ireland so many years ago.

They have been my companions to green valleys where tree fern and wild growth hang lovingly above the banks of trout pools as though to shield them from trespassers. I have gathered much angling wisdom in the thirty-odd years they have been with me. In their agreeable presence many fine men have fished with me; from them knowledge has been gathered. Wherever the angler goes for the first time he is lost without friendly aid and advice from the man who lives on the spot, for he has the advantage that is above all the most valuable — a knowledge of the water. The man who knows the water also knows the fly best adapted to it.

Gratefully I acknowledge the kindness, the hospitality, the expert guidance — often given unobtrusively and never patronisingly — by fellows of the fly rod in almost every corner of this rich and beautiful land.

This is a record of adventures where my "little snobs" have danced on silver reaches in high expectancy.

Failures are not their concern. The man with the rod will often choose the wrong one from his hat or fly-box; they will always play their part.

2. *Snobs on the Riwaka*

If my little "bunch of snobs" had had the choice of a river to
play upon they would surely have chosen the Riwaka in *
Nelson, as I saw it in 1933. On that, my first visit, it gave me
such a warm welcome that I returned at every possible
chance during the following twelve years. On no occasion
was I disappointed with the fishing, and not once was I
obliged to use a wet fly. More than this, the little stream runs
through a rich, warm and sheltered vale in which grow
tobacco, hops, grapes and raspberries which add an exotic
atmosphere. The tightly-knit community seems to have con-
tentment and peace. Many of the people are descended from
pioneer stock who settled there in early colonial days. It has
its village pub – also a family affair – its cricket green, its
small library. To one visitor, anyway, it held endless friend-
liness and charm. It had, of course, delightful fishing waters
where artificial fly only was the permitted form.

My first hour on the Riwaka was after the evening meal
when the last light threw shadows from a big willow on a
calm pool. On my side was the shingly bank so usual there
along most of the reaches. Obviously the pool was deep under
the opposite bank. The stream was shallow at my feet. Little
fish were rising, so it would not be long before better ones
came on. I had tied on a fawny moth with spreadeagle wings
which was dressed to a twelve hook. I noticed a large tabby
cat with Persian fur sitting on the stop-bank behind me. He
ignored my "Hello, puss".

Soon I spotted a good rise on the edge of the shadow and
put the moth up his way. I recall being amused at the noise

this made on the forward throws: "Thrutt, thrutt." It was quite amusing to the cat also, as he strolled down to get a closer look. Afraid of getting hooked up in the willow, I had not managed to get the fly over the fish, but had not put him down. At last he spotted it and took it boldly. He was stronger and wilder than expected, trying the old brownie trick of diving back under the roots of the tree. At last he came splashing noisily to my feet and it was then the cat took part in the business. He pounced into the water and tried to fasten on to the fish. Here was an entirely novel situation that could have cost me my first Riwaka trout. As I always carried a net in those days it was now used to fend puss off till the fish was in the net. At this point the cat disappeared. It seemed I had done something to offend him.

My practice then was always to weigh each fish and record its length. When the job was over I picked up the rod again, found it was hooked in something, heard a commotion and a snarl and found to my horror that I was firmly attached to my busybody feline. Had he swallowed the fishy fly?

After some diplomacy and coaxing I managed to get the big animal in my arms and trace the fly which, it was a relief to find, had not been swallowed but was firmly embedded in the pad of one of his enormous paws.

Now I have always been pleased with my success with that surgery, though the cat was not. Gripping his hindquarters under my left arm and one wrist in each hand I spread him out, belly up, so the only threat to my person was his quite adequate set of fangs. I had to risk his chewing my left ear a bit while I mumbled with my lips along the cast till I was able to grip the hook in my teeth. A final jerk, a startled and angry yowl, and the operation was a complete success. He could probably have done me quite a bit of mischief with his claws, but, being a gentleman, restrained himself, simply finding relief in what he had called me.

Do not imagine that this painful experience cured him. Not so. He was back with me every night after tea. It was probable he would soon be asking for a loan of my rod. To get out of this I had to bribe him with a fish. This he would grab and go tearing off up the bank.

I asked his mistress, Mrs Drummond, about this odd cat.

"Oh, he's used to fishermen. When he gets a fish he brings it home," she replied. "He's a real character."

My daylight fishing on the Riwaka involved much foot-slogging up the river and down again to the hotel. It was better, then, to take a bite of lunch and a bottle of ale to keep myself going on the upper reaches as long as possible.

It was wonderful to be able to get away to a stream like this and investigate it at will; to fish, to bird-watch, to write, to sleep or just to be alone in a lovely New Zealand place. The mind, jaded with the battering of dark trading days of slump, was wiped clean of its weariness and the heart restored with hope after a mere week on a trout stream. Angling has gifts for its devotees that have little to do with the weight of fish in the creel.

On the upper reaches the river is more closely held between its banks. Then rocks are met and some swifter current. Another small stream joins the Riwaka at a spot called the Forks where there are, or were, superb pools for the fly fisher, wet or dry.

A pattern that was working well for me at that time was called the Dad's Favourite with a quill body. This is a short-winged type tied of grey partridge feathers with dark hackles and, of course, the grey quill body. I have seen them only in the South Island, and dressed on a fourteen or twelve hook. Who was "Dad"? It would be nice to know. One can conjure up the image of a small boy naming it in admiration and affection as the fly his father had designed and used to catch a number of fish.

On the Riwaka it was always worth trying a small Hofland's Fancy. This has a dark purple body and brown wings to a size fourteen hook. It rather resembles a flying ant I saw there.

A "believe it or not" experience of mine on the Riwaka indicates what peculiar creatures trout can be. The afternoon was a still and sultry one. The pool was long, deep and fairly wide, with a cut bank opposite a sandy beach. At its head a ridge of big stones formed a barrier over which the stream made a little fall.

The pool, when I reached it, looked as though a couple of hippos had been cavorting there. Banks were wet far from and above normal levels. Some rocks in the cut bank were still dripping. Footmarks of children were everywhere on the beach. There seemed little hope from fishing there.

However, fish it I did, as I had my rod ready and a Dad's Favourite oiled and rarin' to go. Being quite sure that I was simply fooling, I sent the Dad's up into the eye of the pool, where it had barely moved a foot downstream when a big fish pounced on it. The fight he, or rather she — for it was a female — put up was stubborn and hard. At last she came ashore at the bottom of the pool and into my net. She was in perfect order and my Salter scale made her four pounds.

To fish any more that day would have been an anti-climax. Host Bowers also weighed it on the kitchen scales and confirmed the weight as a bit over four pounds, and, with some pride, put it on show for his evening customers.

Now the questions: Where had that fish been all the time those boys had been raising hell in the pool? Had she been there all the time? Did she come up from the lower pool because the water had been stirred up and food made available? And why had no local angler grassed her long before?

If I knew the answer to any one of these questions perhaps I'd be regarded as an ichthyologist instead of being just a simple ichthyolatrist!

When I got back there the following year my good friend Bowers greeted me with: "The fellows in the bar still talk about that four-pound trout of yours."

3. Mr Greenwell's Glory

Many members of the clergy have made notable contributions to the art and literature of angling. It is doubtful whether any of them ever designed a fly to rival the Reverend Greenwell's Glory. This wonderful fly looks simple enough, with its olive floss body, dark-brown wings, slaty hackles and gold ribbing and tail; it is superb in action. So much so that an angler-editor once went on record to state: "If I had to choose but one fly to fish in any part of the world I would unhesitatingly choose Greenwell's Glory."

There was one occasion when I had reason to remember this rather forthright opinion when, during the early days of the Second World War I opened the season with A. G. "Sandy" Monahan and his old friend Frank Paynter.

The morning was bright and clear when they called for me after breakfast at the Riwaka hotel, in Sandy's large car which looked as though it had seen better days. Sandy said the barometer was a bit low, and the weather forecast "not too bright". Nevertheless we were in for "some good fishing where we were going".

In spite of our optimism it was to be a dull opening day for the most part. For some reason or other the fish were completely uninterested in every fly we offered them. Even Frank's small Gold Devon made no impression on them.

This was a puzzling beginning to what, in fact, turned out to be a dramatic day's angling. Though my friends, as local residents, knew the "best places" which had given them good sport at other times, and which appeared to be in first-class order, they could not understand why we had failed.

Sandy decided we should move about twelve miles to a special area where, he averred, the fish always put up a good evening rise. As this was the first day after a seven-month rest, the fishing was certain to be all we could want.

The road was quite good as we drove up to this special spot, but we were not to be so happy about it coming back.

As the evening light began to fade, we came to a fairly large pool below a low fall. Fish started a persistent rise. At least thirty were on the job. On our side there was a sloping bank to the water, giving good room for casting.

Frank fished below; Sandy and I above. There was a hatch of small dark flies to which the fish rose greedily.

Scooping up two or three flies from the surface of the stream and examining them under a pocket lens I decided the nearest artificial in my box was a Black Gnat size twelve; so to my 2x tapered cast one of these was tied with confidence.

Acting on my advice, Sandy tied on a similar pattern.

Then followed an enraging period in which we cast and cast again to the fish and neither of us even touched one. A good fish rose persistently in a wisp of current within nice casting distance. Twice he took the natural alongside my gnat.

"If," I thought, "my fly can be dropped or worked to come down the wisp as close as possible to a natural, the fish might grab them both."

It was a cheeky idea, as I'm not a "dead-eye-dick" caster, but at the second attempt it worked. The two flies were almost touching when my lad rose perfectly and collected them both. Pulling him downstream I managed to keep him there until he turned on his side. He was nearly three pounds.

During the tussle I could hear Sandy calling out things which could not be defined in the rattling of the water over the stones in the lower end of the pool. After I got my fish out it was to find Sandy also with a bent rod. I hurried back up the pool to where I was before. The fish were still feeding and the light had faded.

"Got a Greenwell, Kelly?"

"Yes."

"Try it. Try it!"

Everyone knows the Greenwell's Glory is quite unlike the Black Gnat and is twice the size; but I tied one on and it was accepted almost at once! The fish was a pound and a half.

Sandy landed one and was soon into another. The rise and the fading light made things even more exciting. My third take was landed safely, a nice fish of two and a half pounds.

I could distinguish a good one rising far out of my reach. My Walker rod of seven feet and five and three-quarter ounces was useless for that distance, so I called Sandy down, pointed the spot out and challenged the grand old angler to cover it.

Now Sandy's rod would not have cost more than a fifth of my Walker, and it was made of greenheart. It was ten feet long and must have weighed a pound; but in the old master's hand it was as a feather. To get the height he climbed up on top of a large willow stump about eight feet high where he seemed to balance precariously. It seemed incredible that he could wield his heavy rod and keep his feet.

But there he was, completely in control of the rod and the situation; and, at the second cast, the fish rose in copy-book fashion and was hooked. Yelling like an excited beagle Sandy bounced off his perch and played the fish to a standstill: the heaviest fish of the day, of three and three-quarter pounds.

No exhibition of angling I have ever seen, no book I have ever read has held anything like Sandy's taking of that fish. To my fervid congratulations Sandy replied rather curtly:

"That's all right, Kelly. We'll have to go now. I'd have liked to have taken a 'bag'."

"What do you call a 'bag'?" I asked.

"Five."

"Five! Why that's the smallest limit in New Zealand. Why only five?"

"The idea is to stop Wellington jokers from cleaning out our rivers!"

This, of course, floored me.

Frank rejoined us. It seemed his Gold Devon, which he had used steadily all day with what seemed a rather short line, had been unrewarding.

When we reached the car it was almost pitch dark. We met a biting southerly breeze carrying drifts of sleet.

A tyre was flat!

"Oh, well," said Sandy, "we'll soon change a wheel." Frank and I watched anxiously as one key after another out of a large bunch failed to unlock the boot. Sandy became impatient and I was horrified to see him twisting savagely at what he thought to be the right one.

"Go easy, Sandy," I burst out, "or you'll break that key. It's only phosphor-bronze, you know."

Glaring at me he gritted: "How do you know it's only phosphor-bronze?" and gave an extra twist.

The key twisted off in his fingers.

There we were in a mounting storm locked out of a car on a lonely road, and at least seventeen miles from Motueka. We had not even a torch with which to wave down any passing car.

About an hour went by and we were then pretty wet. Sleet built up on the windscreen and around our feet.

Then headlights appeared and relief seemed at hand. The headlights slowed down to show the driver three wildly waving figures who must have terrified him, for he pushed down his pedal, his engine roared and he tore past us hell bent down the road. The last we saw of him was his red tail-lights turning out of sight in the distance.

"Hell!" said Sandy. "The bastard must think we are drunken hillbillies from Tapawera!"

It was an even longer and more miserable wait before another vehicle came slowing down into sight. This time only Frank stood with his hand up in the glare of the lights.

"Hello, Mr Paynter," a cheerful voice called. "In trouble?"
Frank climbed into the half-ton truck.

"Better go too, Greg," Sandy said. "Frank will take you to
Riwaka pub from his place when he sends a garage man back
with a spare wheel."

"No thanks, Sandy. Babes in the wood should always die
together."

An hour later Frank was back with a mechanic who
opened our car door in about five seconds flat. It did not
seem useful for me to wait any longer, so Frank took me to the
Riwaka Hotel where to my astonishment Mrs Jim, the
proprietor's wife, met me at the door in her dressing gown.

"Thank God you're home," she said fervently. "We've
been so worried that you'd been drowned or something. You
must be nearly dead. Jim gave me the bar keys if you want a
drink. I've turned on a hot bath for you. Go turn it off or it'll
spill over. Did you say you would like a drink? I forget what
you said. I'm so glad you're home. God! What a night! And
it's snowing now."

All this poured from her lips while I stood with water
dripping from my clothes in the middle of her spotless
kitchen. This was happening to *me* in a public house, after
midnight, where I'd been only once since Mrs Jim had been
hostess. It still seems incredible.

A hot bath, two double brandies and sugar, and dry
clobber assured me that I was not dead after all.

Still the astonishing welcome went on:

"I hope you like whitebait fritters, Mr Kelly, I got half a
kerosene tin full this afternoon. Could have got more but got
too cold."

Twice my plate was piled with golden, crisp fritters to
make a meal to remember.

"Now," asked my hostess, "did you get any fish?"

I rolled out my three fine fish with a flourish. Wordlessly
she pounced upon them and, in a matter of seconds, it
seemed, had them cleaned and gutted.

"Where did you learn to do that, Mrs Jim?"

"Ha! Ha! Let me tell you. My father and brothers are commercial fishermen at Picton, "she replied. "I used to go out with them in the boats, even when I was a kid. We all had to work." She laughed delightedly; then sobered in a minute:

"That's why I was so frightened about you tonight. We sea people know about . . ." She faltered and the voice broke. I cut in as quickly as I could:

"I'm sorry you were worried, Mrs Jim. You see, Sandy broke the key of his car and we had to wait." I related the story which restored calmness.

"Here's a hot brandy on the house to go to bed on," Mrs Jim chuckled. "Hope you don't wake up with pneumonia in the morning."

Next morning I woke up to broad daylight. The world was white. The date was October 2, when winter should be well past.

Later as I packed up my fishing clobber which Mrs Jim had dried in her kitchen, I looked at the flies in my hat. There was the battered, bedraggled Greenwell's Glory that had saved the day for me. It was not much to look at. What is the mystery of this fly's attraction for brown trout? Did Mr Greenwell know? Does any other angler know? Do those strange creatures called trout know?

4. A Happy Trio

One of my favourites among the "snobs" is the Coch-y-bondhu. This is a hackle fly, that is, it has no wings. The great thing about the Cochy is its ability to float well, and there are no "upright" wings to worry about. It is useful on a variety of waters, and in my belief the reason for this lies in the likeness it bears to a floating spider from the trout's point of view. Its Welsh history has it that it represents a beetle. This might be correct, but we find the Cochy effective during winter when beetles are off the menu, whereas the spider, being an animal, is around, in vast numbers, for most if not all of the year.

I like the Cochy dressed with a darker hackle than normal because it is easier to see on the water, especially at nightfall. At all times, I find, a little silver on the tail adds greatly to its value. This is no new idea, this silver or gold tip. As long ago as 1720, John Gay gave this couplet to the angling world:

> "Let Nature guide thee. Sometimes golden wire
> The shining bellies of the fly require."

The value of the dark or black-hackled Cochy was confirmed one evening on the Motueka River in the Nelson district about 1942, when I had the good fortune to have once again the company of Sandy Monahan and his friend, Bill Bryant. Both these men were well skilled in the art of dry-fly fishing, and, as they lived there, knew the best reaches on that splendid river.

On this night they chose a fine stretch below the Pangatotara Bridge. As we rigged up our rods my friends watched as I tied on a black Cochy of size eight hook proportions. Sandy asked, "Haven't you a Wickhams Fancy? Why not use one? It's the only one for here, you know."

Then Bill spoke.

"These fish won't even look at that old thing, Greg. Take Sandy's tip or you'll do no good."

"Oh, thanks, fellows. I can't see anything as well as this one; but I'll change if it's no good."

Sandy strode off well downstream to fish up to Bill's chosen pool, which was below me. Both would finally reach the spot where I started.

I went a chain farther towards the bridge where I saw a fish feeding steadily. My first cast was short and I lengthened it slightly. My second offer was accepted and I had a fish tearing line away. I've always had an irresistible urge to let out a wild yell in moments like this. One yell only, then the concentrated silence of effort to get my fish played out. In this case I lost the battle.

"I've lost it, Bill," I called.

"Bad luck, Greg. Perhaps he was foul hooked," he said with a teasing laugh.

"How like a schoolmaster," was all I could think of, which amused Bill even more.

The wading was shallow and, I was told, safe. So my next move was towards a ripple of quicker current where I thought I'd seen a fish. Sure enough there he was, and the black Cochy disappeared in a swirl. This time the yell was deliberately provocative, and this time I landed my fish in a flurry of shallow water at the gravelly edge.

I unhooked my three-pound brown hen fish with considerable pleasure. In another ten minutes I had another of two pounds.

Bill came up to me. "Greg, old boy, have you one of those horrible flies to lend me?"

"Sure thing, Bill. Here's a spare one from my hat."

In the half hour left of fishing time I caught a small one and turned it back with a tale to tell its mother. Both Sandy and Bill had caught one or two each.

They were surprised at my success with the big fly. The Coch-y-bondhu with its black hackle and peacock herl of purple shade with a bit of silver wire on its tail had, in their eyes, achieved the impossible.

My liking for the Coch-y-bondhu was confirmed one afternoon some years later when I came upon a tall doctor from Hamilton casting a large one upstream on a good pool where he was waist-deep in the Whakapapa. The fly looked immense on the dancing current at that time of day.

"Do you like that big Coch-y-bondhu?" I asked.

"Yes," he replied, "I use nothing else, even at Taupo. I say that if they don't like this fly, they can go to hell!"

I saw him on my way back to the cottage. He was still casting industriously.

"Any luck, Doctor?"

"No, not yet."

It seemed that the fish had all gone where he had consigned them.

Whatever North Islanders might think about my little bunch of snobs, they are regarded favourably in Canterbury, Southland, the West Coast and Nelson. In fact, it seems, little snobbies are popular among wet-fly men also on the Mataura, though my South Island adventures were all with the floaters.

My most barren days with the little fellows were near Albert Town where I used them with little purpose on the Hawea and quite so on the Clutha, or Molyneux, as it was then named at that place.

On the last afternoon of that trip, in October, some twenty years ago, my host, Ted Eliot, advised a Red-tipped Governor size eight to be fished downstream. This gave me some excitement and three fish of reasonable size. He took two jacks of about three pounds each, which I remember because of his wife's dry comment about bringing home "those things".

Lake Taupo. Freshly caught trout being prepared for grilling over an open fire

Two 14 lb. rainbow trout caught in Lake Tarawera, Rotorua

Trout fishing at Lake Tarawera, Rotorua

My rather poor rewards in this area of splendid waters can be put down to my lack of knowledge of the water and to sticking too firmly to the use of tiny floating flies.

Now an enormous hydro-electric scheme blots out those grand fishing reaches. It is to be hoped that Nature will restore the fishing by providing areas around the margins of these great dams, though it is difficult to believe that anything can ever replace Nature's own untrammelled streams and rivers.

5. *The Story Behind the Tup*

There is a small stream about <u>seven</u> miles from Timaru. This is the Pareora. As it was wartime when I went there for the first time, transport was not an easy matter. I was lucky enough to find a taxi driver, in times particularly difficult for his trade, who treated me well. He took me to the road bridge — we now call them traffic bridges — and came back for me faithfully at the deadline time that just allowed my catching the north-bound ferry train. What's more, he charged me only fifteen shillings for the entire job, in which he had had to travel thirty miles. I suppose he was sorry for the poor fellow who would go to so much trouble to catch a few little trout that he did not want, and which he liberated as soon as he could.

I walked downstream towards the railway bridge and fished back, using sizes fourteen and sixteen Cochy and Dad's Favourite. By the time I had reached the road bridge five fish from seven to ten inches long had been carefully released and a good many more scared. These small fish seemed to be extremely sensitive to any heavy-booted vibrations and taught me a valuable lesson: fish in clear shallow water are harder to approach than those in deeper water. Another striking thing was that, in these conditions, they were very line shy, or rather, cast shy. Any clumsiness and they were off, leaving torpedo tracks behind them. So, for my first half hour, not even a tiddler rose to take my fly, and I had scared at least twenty. At last I did get a rise from a seven-incher by casting from the side and letting the fly drop on the very edge of the pool. My cast was tapered to 3x to which I added two or three more lengths (natural gut came in about twelve-inch lengths) and I took a good deal more care with my steps before even the smallest trout could be deceived. By the time I got back to the road bridge where the taxi had dropped me I had drawn to the edge five of these bright little fish.

With an hour left I went on above the road bridge where I found the river deeper, with a good pool shouldering a cut bank. "This will be easier," I thought. "More like the Pokai in the Waikato."

Not a fish looked at my Dad's Favourite in half an hour.

"Now, little brothers, as you live in sheep country I'll offer you something special."

As I tried on a size fourteen Tup's Indispensable, I chuckled at the dry wit of its creator, who so named it. The story had been related to me many years before by a chalk-streamer.

"You notice the peculiar pink of the wool in the body? How warm it is, and, because it is naturally greased, that it needs no additions. The only place this wool is found is on the essential appendage of a ram, which in my country is a tup. Hence Tup's Indispensable."

As a result of this story I sent to Farlow, London, and got a dozen from Mr W. A. Hunter, the manager, and author of *Fisherman's Knots and Wrinkles*. It was one of these I now bent on to interest the little fish of the sheep country. Before the taxi came back I had six more of Pareora's citizens to unhook and steady in the water until they caught up their wind and swam away with an incredible tale to tell.

When Captain Hamilton wrote *Trout-fishing and Sport in Maoriland* (N Z Government Printer, 1904) he listed the Pareora as having thirty-three miles of angling water: "Banks mostly low and clear in the lower reaches, then being rocky in the gorge. Wadeable mostly. Landing mostly good. Brown trout."

On subsequent visits to this river I found the Tups as good on the upper reaches as on the lower ones, but heavier trout and faster currents cost both fish and fly on several occasions.

The drawback with these wee flies is the difficulty in seeing them on broken currents. They can, of course, be fished down as wets when visibility is not important.

When last I saw the Pareora in March, 1965, at the road bridge where I had started so long ago, I was dismayed to find it reduced to a slight and not very clean trickle. It appeared that the "Indian sign" was on it. I was glad it had not been my intention to fish it, as it was a sorry sight. I am much cheered to read in George Ferris's *The Trout are Rising* (Heinemann) which was published in 1964, that the Pareora is still a lovely stream with a natural reproduction of a high order. He adds that, like the Mataura, it maintains a steady balance of good fish year by year.

All anglers who know the Pareora will echo that author's hope that this will remain so for many seasons to come.

6. One Can Never Tell

One fine spring morning about eight o'clock, Messrs McRae and Berry — both Ernies — picked me up at the Club Hotel in Timaru for a planned day's fishing on the Opihi River. The Opihi was, they said, long past its best, but was still fishing well.

For years it was celebrated as one of the most productive streams in Canterbury, and that was high praise indeed. So, on this my first visit, I was excited as we travelled through pleasant farmlands on our way to their chosen piece of the famous stream. I was in the pleasant company of men with whom I had fished before. They were both expert with the trout rod.

"What's the limit, boys?"

The following silence reddened my ears.

"We don't know about limits," Mac gritted. "Sometimes we are glad to get a couple."

"Oh. I just wondered," I said. "Never exceed three fish myself."

After going through several gates, we stopped on the top of a cut bank and I had my first view of the Opihi. At this point there was a large and deep-looking pool on my left below a wide ripple.

"That's my spot for a start, I hope," I thought. It was.

My friends were into their thigh boots and ready for the fray in a few minutes, whereas I had to drag myself into ponderous armpit waders, with their outside socks and brogues. As I fitted on my quill-bodied Greenwell's Glory, I deferred to Mac: "This fly all right for here?"

"Yes, quite good. Trim those wings back a little and clip out as much hackle as you can. Just leave enough so the fly will float."

This advice, from one of the masters of the art, has stood me in good stead ever since. Nearly all shop flies are over-dressed.

My friends disappeared, leaving me the pool I had chosen. I climbed down the bank. As soon as I started casting and before the angles of the current could be worked out, a blast of hot air hit my left cheek. In a matter of seconds a shattering dry storm struck about me like an explosion. My line was lifted, torn would be the better term, off the water and the fly cracked like a whip overhead, and there was no abatement.

I climbed up the bank to look at what was coming and was almost blinded with dust. Stones and small sticks lashed my face. Creeping back I crouched under the cut bank to wonder at such elemental ferocity. I was soon joined by the other two. There we sat, dismayed. Above us a herd of two-year-old steers stampeded, bawling with fear and shaking the bank.

"Hell let loose!" was Mac's unimaginative remark.

Hoping the storm would pass or abate enough for us to carry on fishing, we huddled under that high bank for about two hours. During this time we devoured a gritty lunch, peeling back the wrappings gingerly and snatching a mouthful.

In the end we gave in to the conditions, dismantled our rods, changed back into normal footwear and battled our way back to the car. Ernie Berry drove back in the teeth of the storm, with thick dust and gravel blasting against the windscreen. None of us had anything to say. It paid to keep one's mouth shut.

My next opportunity to fish a mid-Canterbury river provided another surprise.

On my way south I saw that all the rivers were badly

stained. So it was in poor spirits that I called at England, McRae Ltd in Timaru to moan in Mac's ear.

"Why not try the Ohape? Do you know the Ohape?"

"I do not. I've heard of Taihape on a Saturdee night though."

"Yes, I heard that one during the war in France," he laughed. "Now just a tick." He dived into his office and came out beaming.

"Thought so. My machine expert has a plant to install out that way. He's going today, now, instead of tomorrow and will drop you at the Ohape bridge. You fish upstream, of course, and meet him higher up. The job will take two hours or so and you should get some fun. Use small flies."

The expert called for me at the little pub where I always stayed. He had his nine-year-old daughter with him. To my teasing "What? No school today?" she made no reply.

"She's not been well."

Nothing more was said till we stopped on the Ohape bridge. I saw a narrow ribbon of water that was as clear as water can be.

"Funny that this stream is clear when the Orari is flooded. Don't you think so?"

"Must be spring fed."

"What a blockhead I am. Of course that's it."

So for me this day became historic – the only occasion I was to get angling of the chalk-stream type. There was a clear, cold waterway winding endlessly across open meadows with banks heavily fringed with tall native grasses. Sedges, toetoe and flax, docks with occasional foxglove and penny-royal all seemed ready to add to the excitement of casting.

For most of the afternoon it was all hands and knees. To stand erect was to put every trout indoors and under the bed. The water level was at least three feet below ground level. So a six-foot man's hat was nine feet high. The reaches, if they could be called such, were short, and long casting was impossible, as the stream twisted and turned almost to double round on itself. The plan was to keep low, take advantage of the growths and flick the fly high in the air and let it fall. Many casts were bungled and at least six flies left to their fate.

Two odd impressions registered: the lazy rise made slow-motion pictures of the take and the confident acceptance of the fly.

At a point just near a left-hand bend a large flax bush looked to be the place for a quick meal. Before I could move forward my eye caught the outward ripples of a ring made by a rising fish. He was partly obscured by the flax so to cover him it was necessary that the fly should be flicked round the corner. Care had to be taken to get outside the outer leaves of the flax bush; something almost beyond my ability, but at least I could try it.

I moved forward on my knees, now sore, keeping the fly going high above. I was just about to let it go when the ground burst in my face, and a blast of air nearly lifted off my hat.

I had crawled right up on a grey duck which was sitting on a clutch of eggs. She had stuck it out till I was nearly on top of her, then shrieking like a banshee at midnight, she ripped up past my face giving me the devil's own fright. At once she returned and, quacking weakly, fell into the water with at least one broken wing and a couple of badly injured legs. Next she was out on the grass gasping and staggering, falling one way and then the other. Sure! She was the dyingest and easiest-to-be-caught wild fowl in the world.

"Only come and catch me, man. I'll make you a lovely dinner; I'm young and fat. Come on, come on."

"Go on, you silly old bitch. Stop your fooling. I'll not touch your nest."

I recovered my rod and saved my fly. My brave wild duck flew high up and down until she saw I was a few chains away from her nest below the flax. She then disappeared from my sight and I knew she had sneaked back to her domestic responsibilities.

Of the eleven grassed only one was kept, and she was a lovely one of one and three-quarter pounds. She, too, would have been released had the engineer been alone. The little girl took it without a word, and held it on her knee all the way home. Every now and then she would fold back the damp sugarbag wrapping to stare at her present before rewrapping it carefully. Whether her idea was to have it for tea or whether she was sorry the pretty thing was dead, I shall never know.

Her father had no interest in angling and could not appreciate how much pleasure his kindness had made possible.

If I learnt one thing that day it was to understand why Timaru anglers are devoted to dry-fly fishing and why so many South Islanders are dabsters at the art.

7. The Dry-fly Angler's Paradise

Between 1933 and 1948 was possible for me to sample the trout fishing near Invercargill. Though the visits were few, they held vivid enough experiences for me to understand the popularity of the dry fly on rivers there so well suited to its use.

There are few trout rivers anywhere that do not run down pleasant places, but if no fish had been caught on my first visit to the Otapiri in 1938, the loveliness of this valley would have been enough.

My two companions, Lester Whelam and Jim Robertson, gave me some guidance regarding flies and where to go.

"Use small dry flies," advised Lester, "and keep out of sight as much as possible."

The former was easy enough, as I had plenty of sizes ten, twelve, fourteen and sixteen, but to keep out of sight on the clear green pastureland banks was another matter. Luckily I was left to my own devices and could moon about as much as I pleased.

I found one long gravel-bottomed reach with fair-sized boulders here and there. The water was rather leisurely as it burbled past me, reminiscent of a small boy jumping down the steps of a grandstand. Jump, pause and look, jump again.

Trout of about twelve inches were common in little dishes of water below boulders. They looked easy, but they were not. My casting was weak and inaccurate so I muffed chances. For all that, I managed to bring these lively little fellows to the edge. Not one was, I thought, big enough to kill.

At the top of the reach I sat down in a shady spot watching the life around me. Native birds were feeding in the flowering trees; a yellow weasel cantered along the edge of the water on the other side of the stream. He made a pleasing picture of a lithe hunter at work; he was quite unaware of me. So was my next visitor, a splendid hare who loped down along the opposite bank, stopped, sat up and then looked at me gravely. I knew I was not regarded as anything unusual when the animal started to preen itself before quietly loping away. It is odd how these small matters stick on the mental image of past events.

When my friends came back to find me, they had many fish, which made my single two-and-a-half pounder look inadequate, though they thought it a fine one for the Otapiri.

A trip to the Mimihau at Wyndham is remembered for its active reaches and stout little fighting brownies. The fact that these fish were the most vigorous of fighters made me wonder if climate has anything to do with it. The farther south one goes, the more "go" the brown trout has. What else but the colder climate can account for this? I'll go further and state that the North Island brownies, though bigger as a general rule, are dull actors. They tend to bore down along the bottom in a dogged drag and will snag themselves around a rock or root quite cunningly, wheareas those southern brownies leap and rip with almost the same determination as a rainbow, making their landing a much more interesting contest.

If this opinion, based admittedly on limited experience, is reasonable, it is quite surprising to find southern anglers using very small hooks. One evening, on one of my visits to Invercargill, I called as usual on my friends the Hamilton brothers who had gathered around them a small party of anglers. They were celebrating, informally, the success of their day fishing the Mataura. Their angler guests for the day were American VIPS. All had had wonderful fishing and all had caught fish. The tiger of the party was, as usual, Lester Whelam with a fine bag of up to two-and-a-half pounders.

"What did you catch those fish on, Lester?" I asked, VIPS and gin forgotten.

"Size eighteens, Greg. Nothing any bigger was of use today on that water."

"Size eighteen? That's the smallest hook I know." Yet he had taken at least ten fish!

The only way to convey the minuteness of the eighteen is to point out that the bight of the hook is $\frac{3}{32}$ of an inch and its entire length not quite a quarter of an inch.

Hunting through my old fly-box, I found a quill-bodied Coch-y-bondhu in this size. I remember using it only once and that was on the Wainuiomata near Wellington where it was ineffective.

Last week a Taupo friend of mine, who is a keen angler and who runs a nice Doric burr or two, exclaimed when I showed him this and some other little snobs: "Wha' are they forr-r? Don't tell me you catch *troot* on them!"

No one is likely to reach the conclusion that Southland trout are all small by North Island standards. Even in rivers I have mentioned, such as the Makarewa, big fish are caught late in the evening on large flies tied to heavy nylon casts. In lakes like Mavora and Manapouri fish of five to eight pounds are not phenomenal.

One of New Zealand's distinguished visitors, Dr J. C. Mottram, has this to say of Lake Te Anau in his book *Fly Fishing: Some New Arts and Mysteries* (The Field Press, 1921): "Great brown trout live in the lake. These ascend the river, and finding pleasant quarters here, sheltering under submerged trees, feeding on the insects dropped from the foliage above and on the quantities of ephemeridae which live among the stones and the moss on the river-bed. These fish, instead of returning to the lake, settle down to spend the summer in the river. They have been wooed by many kinds of flies and baits, but only by the net have they been brought to the bank. Nevertheless, it is impossible to persuade the angler not to fish, if he has once seen these grand fish in the crystal water."

8. The Big One that Did Not Get Away

According to our non-angling friends, this is something that never happens. That the big fish always escapes is one of their harmless and rather senile jokes.

When we come to consider the matter, it is not unnatural for the extra large trout to escape. Sensibly, most anglers use the lightest gear they can get away with for the water they are covering. Were they to use a big hook on a thick line or cast strong enough to make sure of a big one, the average trout would not be fooled.

So, the better plan is to "fish fine" for the more usual sizes. Inevitably something big will be hooked sooner or later, with the risk of broken tackle. Sometimes, of course, extra skill and great good luck make the landing possible; but the more natural result is a break, which merely goes to reinforce the hoary joke.

Sad to say, there is often a bit of a sneer in this aged witticism. Did the angler's imagination enlarge the one he lost? He cannot produce the big one. All he can produce is the story, in which the fish can be just as big as he feels like making it.

Of course the biggest ones get away. Any fool should know that, even non-anglers.

It should be admitted that my twelve-pounder was not, for that date, so very, very big in 1927, the period of the big ones at Taupo; but this was my biggest then, and forty years later he still remains so. It should be admitted further his luck was right out, firstly to be hooked at all, and secondly, to be raked out of the water.

Two of us had had a fortnight deerstalking in the Urewera country and were on our way home to Auckland. My friend Mappin, now Sir Frank, knew of a spot on the Waikato River near Taupo. This was called the Huka Falls water and was already famous.

A pretty little stream of thermal water bubbled out of the hill above the camp, cascading over a lip to form a bathing pool under a fall. There was room only for one person at a time. Dense tea-tree and fern screened the pool to make it private.

This was marvellous for us after the freezing creek water in the Urewera, where, as it was very shallow, the only thing we could do was to lie down in it.

Mapp got some extra fun at my expense in both places by pitching a bucket of cold water over me just as I finished drying my shivering body. I never could quite catch him in the same way.

But back to the Big One. The small telescopic steel rod I had packed in my shooting kit served well enough on the banks of the Rangitaiki at Kopuriki where I caught a few small fish of about a pound. This rod was useless on the Huka Falls pools, so I hired the best I could get from a Taupo dealer on the wharf in the village. This man, Mr Laughlan, ran boats for hire, did some kind of tourist service and was generally the source and fountain of knowledge for the whole district. The best rod he had was a light and flimsy-looking greenheart of Alcock's make. It was almost as dicky, I thought, as my steel one. However, it was to serve me well.

My mate caught a nice three-pound rainbow the first evening after I had given up to get the tea ready.

The night was full of stars and a soft current of the water breeze swayed the tall tea-tree across the sky. Life was very sweet. Not far away the great Huka Falls filled the air with their might, to warn anglers not to take liberties.

Next day we drove to Broadlands to see the bird sanctuary established there by Mr E. E. Vaile, the great pioneer of

pumice farming and my companion's friend. When we
returned it was to find two other rods fishing "our" water.
One of these was a Canadian tourist who was using a Hardy
"Hi-Regan" rod of salmon proportions. His whole equip-
ment was of similar expensiveness. I was glad that my outfit
was not in view.

"How's the fishing?" I ventured.

"Rotten," he growled. "I'm disappointed. My friend and I
have bin here two hours for nothing." He rolled up and
followed his mate who had already departed.

There was a natural platform of rock just above the pool
where I started to fish. The river was very deep at this point
and was straight down below me. The water was, perhaps,
five feet from the top of my platform. I had no net so had to
make a gaff (then legal) out of fencing wire lashed to a stick.

My line was a greased tapered number three to which I
had spliced a hundred yards of braided silk. Except for the
cast, a grilse, also tapered, which Hardy listed as five/five
strength, my line was for dry-fly work. The fly, a Ewe Wasp,
though out of date in 1967, was all the go then. A single
specimen remains in my assortment of oddities. Here is the
dressing: body, mohair black for two-thirds of length of hook,
and yellow for rear one-third; binding, medium silver tinsel;
hackle, black and sparse and underneath hook (not a collar);
tail whisks from neck of golden pheasant; wings from cock
pheasant's rump. The wings are slim.

Where the name Ewe Wasp originated was never explained, and if a Ram Wasp existed I have never heard of it.

Why this fly lost its popularity is also a mystery. Perhaps
some pundit discovered she was barren.

Following the usual pattern for Taupo angling then I cast
across and let the current bear the line downstream. Of
course the line would not sink though the fly and cast did to
some extent.

This sort of threshing can become very boring when
nothing is happening and I was beginning to agree with what

Mrs Ted Webber with fish caught in
Tukituki River, Hawkes Bay

The Buller River

Upper Waitahanui, Lake Taupo

the Canadian had said when I noticed a small worm-like thing in a little pool of water on the platform not far from where I was standing. "Surely," I thought, "Taupo anglers don't stoop to using worms here!"

I picked the thing up. It was not a worm at all. It was a two-inch length of lead wire.

"Ho, ho!" says I, "Ho, ho! Now get thee behind me, Satan."

Satan was not co-operative, so the lead wire found itself wound round my cast above the third blood-knot, and the Ewe Wasp plopped into the water at my feet and spiralled down in great style. It might have been out of sight when I saw a great fish diving to where it should have been. Instinctively, I raised my rod sharply to feel the jolt that fills the heart with joy, and which, at the same time, turns the stomach over.

Almost at once something that looked like a flitch of bright bacon leapt out of the water with frightening vigour. Then he took off upstream leaping and leaping again.

It was impossible to follow the fish either up or down for more than a few yards, because the bushes grew to the edge.

When he came back he would, I knew, beat me if he got away downstream any distance. As it was, my little cheap greenheart rod was hooped like a garden arch and was expected to break in two any second. But, as it was a matter of "pull devil pull baker", it was a smashed rod or nothing. I yelled to Mapp for help but because of the little waterfall near the camp he could not hear.

Then the fish started to swim in dogged circles round and round over a radius of twenty to thirty yards with occasional ripping runs of a chain or two. Oddly, he always flashed up against the current.

When finally he gave up the battle and turned on his side below me, I tried to gaff him. All the beastly wire did was to scrape him harshly and send him mad again. However, he was done and when the wire was worked carefully under one

D

of his gills it did the job. I slid the big fellow up on to the ledge at my feet where I fell on him to make sure.

I looked at my watch; it was a quarter to four. It was twenty minutes past three when I found the lead wire. So that struggle had lasted a full twenty-five minutes.

When I got back to camp Mapp was frying something, I forget what. I threw the fish on the ground where it fell with a thump. The pan was left to look after itself as Mapp walked round the big fish three times without a word.

I offered this fish to him as his family table was bigger than mine, but he would not accept it. He did accept one I caught next morning before we left for home. It was a mere nine-pounder. If my good old mate ever reads this yarn, it will be his first knowledge of its rather ignominious capture.

I might say, in justice to myself, that the second fish was caught by fairer means. And in justice to the Canadian it was not his lead.

Changes have taken place along that stretch of the Waikato. Some years after these events Alan Pye opened his famous Huka Lodge where he still lives in retirement with his wife. The little warm stream we camped on is now used by the Pyes to heat their greenhouse in which they grow magnificent begonias. As well, Alan is widely famed as a grower of narcissi.

But anglers know the man best for his skill as a master of the fly rod. After Alan took over this property, now one of the loveliest spots on the river, the fame of the Huka water spread far and wide. People from all over the world called there, some of them to come time and time again.

The place is still providing some good sport though with the development of hydro schemes the fishing has faded to a shadow of what it once was. For all that, it recently revived some of its former lustre as being the place in New Zealand where Her Majesty the Queen Mother landed the only trout of her tour.

9. *Broad Hint to Glory*

It was more or less of an accident that the hint was dropped. Andrew Dobson was famous as one of the greatest masters of a shotgun in his day; but no one seemed to know anything about his skill with a trout rod. My accidental discovery was made when I showed him a photograph of the twelve-pound rainbow which I'd caught a few weeks earlier in Taupo.

"Aye," said Andrew, "a fine fish it is. Aye. It's bigger than any I've ever caught."

"Oh, I didn't know you were an angler, Andrew. Where do you go?"

"Tae Kakahi."

"Have any luck there?"

"Och. Onybody can catch troot there," he replied with a Scot's modesty. "Got eleven last time."

"What! In one day?"

"Wasna a whole day. But a fair time."

"How do you get there?" I asked, knowing he had no car.

"Catch a goods train fra Taumarunui about ten. Aboot an hoor later you are at Kakahi station. It's aboot a mile to yon river. Another slow train leaves for Taumarunui at six or so."

"Dry fly, Andrew?"

"Dry or wet whichever," he answered. "But sma' ones are best."

The rod took me briefly to Rotoiti, Rotorua, and, when my job demanded it, to South Island waters. An odd hour snatched at Manunui and Taumarunui itself had to satisfy me.

But one day I got a chance at the Kakahi water. I walked

to the village store and asked Mr Pratt if he knew a handy spot.

"The Whakapapa is dirty," he said. "Go to the Wanganui. It's about three miles farther. Go over the bridge near the cookhouse and follow the bush tramline up for half a mile. You get some great water there. Have to scramble down the bank."

I had not moved very far from the store when my surroundings were gripped with a strange silence and stillness. Within ten minutes I was in a jungle of tea-tree through which the wheel marks twisted and turned along a brownish pumice "road" which threw up a strong odour of decaying humus. Two forms of movement were there: slight wisps of steam from the warm scrub and restlessly flitting fantails. All else held its breath.

From the ten foot high tea-tree the track suddenly emerged and I was at the cutting that ran down to the water.

And this was something quite different. The story goes that some visionaries conceived the idea of building a railway line from Kakahi to Taupo, and this cutting was just a start of the earthworks. Being pure pumice, with little fear of slipping, the sides were almost perpendicular. The ever-growing tea-tree adorning the tops bent across until they almost met, giving an engaging tunnel-like effect.

At the bottom a surprisingly strong and broad river met me. A foot-wide track led to a swing bridge from the middle of which exciting trout water was to be seen in both directions.

The silence of the plateau was gone. In its place was the endless murmur of swirling water whose conversations I was to learn thoroughly in studying the varying moods of that fascinating river, the Whakapapa.

Upstream, the logging people had built a bridge which had a rugged and exciting personality of its own. It was simply two tree trunks laid side by side with the round tops chopped flat so the wheels would not sideslip. There was no planking.

The driver had to be good enough to steer his articulated truck with its tons of logs so accurately that no undesirable incident happened. These two logs had to be sixty or seventy feet long, and were fitted into rock and concrete abutments at each end. Steel hawsers were attached at one end. When a big flood broke the abutments at the thin end of the logs, the water simply swung them aside and the hawsers held them securely until the stream's rage abated. After that a tractor dragged them back.

From the swing bridge the track veered to the left through a grove of young totara trees, tall, straight limbed and of the darkest green. With them stood odd grey birch and lace-barks, tall ponga ferns each one of which leaned towards the trackway for the light. So dense was the undergrowth that the absurd thought obtruded, "If the trees tried to walk, they would soon trip in this tangle."

Suddenly, I was faced with another stream, over which there was no bridge. This, I afterwards learned, was the right-hand branch of the Whakapapa.

The trucks had to ford this branch, and I had to do the same. This involved changing to waders and re-changing on the other bank. I learnt an important lesson; though the stream was only eighteen inches or so deep, the pull of the current was so strong that a careless step would have meant disaster.

Once over the ford and up the bank, I saw the range of hills forming the far bank of the Wanganui. At three points high black-grey cliffs stood framed in the green of the forest.

I was closer to the Wanganui than expected, and was sure some good fishing pools were to be found there; but Mr Pratt had given me clear directions and it would have been churlish to disregard them. So, on the way across the open, though scrub covered levels, for another mile or so until a second swing bridge was found. Across this I came to a mill cookhouse and turned upstream along a railway line built by the sawmillers for the sole purpose of getting their logs down from the far bush workings. I left the line and scrambled along an old logging track until still another of these "bushman" swing bridges appeared.

From the approach to the structure, now rotten and quite beyond service, I got a good view of the pool to which the storekeeper had sent me.

The water was quite clear. This was peculiar after the unfishable condition of the Whakapapa as I had seen it a few minutes earlier; but understandable when it was remembered that this stream came from a distant watershed, the Tongariro mountain, where, owing to its lesser height, ice fields were thinner than those on Ruapehu where the Whakapapa had its birth.

In this midday warmth the hum of insects seemed louder than the sound of the stream. It was completely different from its neighbour. Here was dry-fly water for hours. But how to get to it?

Then I spotted them! They were lying on the opposite side of the pool, up near the bridge. They appeared immense in that clear water, lying in a quite shallow place, one behind another in a long line, a dozen at least. I judged them as three to five pounds in weight.

If I could only get across there! The bridge, with rotting boards, linked by a nail or staple to the suspending wires sixty feet above the river was not inviting, so I battled my way about half-way down the long pool to a large rock on its edge.

A tip I once picked up from an old fishing book was: "When you reach any water, sit down for ten minutes before you try to fish it. This gives the trout, who must be aware of some vibration caused by your approach, time to settle down again." So, at this point, I sat down to eat my almost forgotten sandwiches and to empty my tea flask.

Time was running out, as it always does with me, and I had a fair walk back to catch my train. It was now, or not at all. The far too luxuriant growth of ferns and wineberry made back casting impossible. All that could be done was to switch right and left up and downstream, and flick the fly outward on the last upstream throw.

This was possible with the light cane rod of seven and a half feet (five and three-quarter ounces) and a number three tapered line with cast also tapered to 2x. The split-wing Red-tipped Governor, oiled and with wings pulled apart, made its first perilous journey and sailed almost out of sight before being picked up gingerly and worked out again. I had very little confidence in this manoeuvre, as the fly was not far enough out in the stream nor yet far enough upstream, but on the second journey an incredible thing happened: a rainbow swam upward out of the deep water and confidently accepted the Governor, to be well and truly hooked. This was the most graceful take of a dry fly I have experienced. That, perhaps, is why every detail of its taking, and of the battle which followed, is remembered.

Luck and hook held. The clear, open, snagless pool and my height above the water gave me the necessary advantage. The fish helped, as the rainbow always does, by exhausting herself with brainless leaps out of the water, until finally she turned her lovely silver and red side to the sunlight and was thankfully drawn out. A short, thick and perfectly shaped four-pound hen.

Such was the introduction to glory. It was the beginning of many years of magnificent sport. The highland air of the mountain country, the sweet smell of the rich forest with its groves of splendid totara trees, the dark-blue bluffs below which rare blue ducks sported fearlessly, the white stillness of high pumice banks under which trout pools curled and gurgled. Where birdlife was orchestral in dawn light. Where, in winter, crisp white morning reflected the clear warm sunlight.

There I was to build my little fishing house. There I found consolation and restoration after terrible days of grief and worry. And there also on retirement my dear wife and I built a permanent home.

Splendid castles called mountains; rugged hills and round peaks that caught the first rays on days almost always sunny. Where the ruru owl called at night to the loneliness of the past with a note of hope and cheer. Wonderful days and nights of fishing the gallant waters. Dry-fly fishing to satisfy the most ardent devotee of that weird and often misunderstood art. Kakahi.

10. *The Best Fly for the Water and Season*

Most of us have found out by experience the importance of knowing what is the best fly for the water and season. Though standard patterns like the Greenwell's Glory, Black Gnat, Red-tipped Governor, Coch-y-bondhu and some others have a wide application, there are special flies to excel them in some places when used at the correct time.

Among these, for the Taumarunui district, is one known far and wide as the Twilight Beauty. I first met it in Kaitieke about 1940.

Mr Fred Crocker had invited me to come up from Wellington to open the season with him and his brothers on the Retaruke River. The Kaitieke Valley lies about a dozen miles west of the main railway line between Raurimu and Owhango and can be reached from both these points. The Retaruke rises west of Owhango and flows south-westward to join the Wanganui at Wades Landing. Where I met it, and fished it with Fred and his brothers, the river lies along the valley, slow flowing, tree lined and not entirely clear of stain. As far as I know this water, there is nothing but brown trout in it.

The fisherman's rule – "Small fly for small water" – appeared to apply, at least where I started. So I chose a size twelve Black Gnat with the idea that it would suit the slightly coloured water. All I got for an hour's diligent casting were two twelve-inch bull-headed males. Fred was doing better, as one of his was a two-pounder. The elder brother, Charles, who had a dairy herd and was late on the scene, surprised me by producing a size-ten hooked pitch black

fly which he named Twilight Beauty and which he had tied
himself.

"This is the best fly for here and at Kakahi," he remarked
as he caught me looking sideways at it. "In fact, it was
invented down there."

He took one out of a match box and handed it to me. It
looked a pretty rough job. I stuck it in my hat and thanked
him. I had no intention of using it.

"I tie these myself. All you need to do is get some black
cotton and shoot a blackbird."

By the time I met him again my hat had quite a few more
flies stuck in it. They were the ones I had tried without result.

It was almost lunch time, and as the boys had to help their
father with lamb docking in the afternoon, my one day on the
Retaruke looked like ending poorly. Then I saw a fairly large
fish cruising round and round a dam-like little pool. The
surface was almost glassy. The fish was swimming in a circle
picking up flies and beetles off the surface. It seemed to me
that when he saw something on the surface in his path, he
wagged his tail like a pleased puppy as he rose to take it. For
ten minutes or so, from behind a bush, I had cast my
Coch-y-bondhu ahead of him; but he ignored it.

"Don't cast ahead of him. Cast behind him. Put on my
Twilight. After he passes your bush chuck the fly at his tail."

This seemed silly advice, but I was a guest and had to con-
form. I mounted his monstrous black beastie, slopped it with
oil, and "chucked" it behind him. Nothing happened.
"Leave it on the water. He might see it next time round."

To my utter astonishment the fish, wiggling his tail
happily, came round again, was almost past the monster,
turned back and fairly jumped on it. He was a full foot under
water before I had the wit to whip up my rod. Needless to
say, I had him.

This trick of casting behind a cruising fish has been tried a
few times since that day. Sometimes it has worked and sometimes it has not. But one thing is certain; unless the water is

almost dead still, there will be the fatal drag on the fly before the fish has time to stroll round to it again.

Apart from this consideration, the doubt still remains in my mind as to whether that cruiser would have taken any other fly if he had seen it. He had passed by the Cochy, but might not have seen the tiny thing. He could not have failed to see Charlie's monster.

That afternoon we had something else to think about besides fish. We were all mixed up with ewes, lambs, dogs and dust in the sheepyards on one of the hottest days I have ever felt.

There was not a breath of wind in the basin where the yards were built, and the sun poured down into it making a heat trap. All that, and the work of catching the vigorous lambs, carrying them to the operating table where Mr Crocker did the necessary surgery, treating wounds and releasing lambs outside the yards, is well remembered by one of the party to this day.

Next day, in the afternoon, we went to Kakahi twenty miles away. Charlie caught three good fish, all on his funny Twilight fly. I had only one, and that, though four pounds, fell for a brown moth pattern that I drifted down over a bit of a rill. It was the only fish I saw. I had not used the big fly that Charlie had given me.

The Twilight Beauty is now used by thousands of anglers and has joined the distinguished group of standards such as the Greenwell's Glory, Coch-y-bondhu, Red-tipped Governor and so on.

The story of its development was learned quite by accident when I was invited to write something about the fishing of the Kakahi district for a school jubilee booklet. The editor, a woman, still lives in the district and was a pupil at the little school "in the days when everybody went fishing", and Mr Basil Humphrey became postmaster. As a dry-fly angler this man would have revelled in the kind of fishing then available. My informant, Mrs Mont-Brown of Owhango, tells how he

decided that New Zealand trout were worthy of New
Zealand flies. So he set about catching living creatures he
discovered about the rivers, those taken on the wing being
most enlightening.

Apparently Mr Humphrey interested other locals in his
researches. They brought him good specimens. These were
examined, contrasted and discussed by all. Difficulties were
experienced in finding and getting suitable feathers for the
patterns decided upon, but, with patience, these were overcome and several patterns were evolved. All experimental
flies were tried out by the members of this little circle, which,
by the way, included Mrs Mont-Brown's father, Mr Freeman, until finally two of our now famous New Zealand
patterns emerged. Mr Humphrey claimed one was a beauty
especially in the twilight when "the rise" was on, and so was
named our Twilight Beauty, a copy of which is rarely absent
from my hat.

Another fly that has made a name for itself in many places—
I have seen it being used on the Otipiri in Southland – was
evolved by that same small band of enthusiastic anglers at
Kakahi. It was named after the ten-year-old daughter of Mr
Freeman by their leader and has been known in its several
forms ever since as the Jessie. The possibility is that little
Jessie Freeman was one of the keenest of those people who
were searching for and catching insects on the wing. This is
fairly plain when we see how vividly she, as Mrs Mont-
Brown, remembers the activities and history of that little
band of fifty years ago.

My correspondent adds that the Kakahi Queen was a very
popular pattern in that district for many years, but does not
claim that it was the work of the Humphrey coterie.

11. The Apron Pool

If I had called it "the Shrine" instead of "the Apron" it would have been nearer the truth. The naming of the pool was simple; the hooking of a trout in it was not.

One moonlight night I looked down on that length of the Whakapapa from a sixty foot high pumice bank to see a small waterfall shining snow white below. It looked like an apron spread wide, as it splashed over a bench of boulders.

Next day I made up my mind to investigate it. Crossing the stream by a shaky swing bridge below it and looking down on the pool, I saw that it had been made by a freak flood. Actually the pool had resulted from a splitting of the stream by a small island so that one half, the left, looking downstream, ran straight and swiftly many feet lower than the other half. The fall was made when the right-hand half was forced by its bank to turn left again to rejoin its neighbour. In doing so it tumbled its full width over the freak bench of boulders.

Where the two rejoined, their combined force had gouged out a deep hole at the very head of the pool to form a perfect "lie" for feeding fish.

Below the "eye" the pool spread out attractively and, over its sixty or seventy feet length, gradually shallowed under the bridge to another similar waterfall.

This water was of little value for wet-fly fishermen and useless for the bait caster. But the dry-fly man who knew its secrets could have wonderful sport there. It was my good fortune to discover these secrets; and for twelve or thirteen years it treated me with unstinted generosity. In fact, when we came to live there, one of my wife's friends, on one of her visits to us, described it as "K's cool storage pool".

Many people fished the Apron but as far as I could learn, few had caught much in it. The reason for failure was their approach. Wet-fly men could not move down the straight run on the left, as the water was far too fast for this. They were forced to come to the head of the pool down the other branch, and would emerge on the boulders at the very head, below which the fish were lying. And as the boulders were several feet above the general level of the pool, they could be seen by all the fish in it.

The upstream angler could not approach the pool's "hot spot" from straight below because the water was too close to a cut bank and too deep anyway. He had to come round the end of this bank and move to the river from the side. Unless he got down on hands and knees, the fish at the lower end would see him and bolt up among the others. Then all, on the alert, would stay below the surface and refuse any fly.

It was my lesson on the Pareora that taught me the importance of the cunning approach. So, to get at the fish without being spotted I cut a "secret" track through the growth on the bank to the edge and, lowering the rod, reel first, worked down the cut bank by way of a few projecting tree roots to a small shelf at water level. From there it was easy to move cautiously forward along the lip of the fall to cast a fly under, or close to, the edge of the Apron. Here was the lie of the trout, in an area of water about twelve feet long and about four feet wide, water that held a fair prospect of a rise to a properly delivered fly.

Many times indeed, when extra care was taken and everything appeared to be favourable, there would be no response. On other occasions fish would rise, be hooked, played and lost. Many a fish has got out too far and, aided by the swift water, too far down the pool to wind back. There was absolutely no way of following. On one of these days my good friend T. C. was with me when I hooked a lovely four-pound rainbow on a size twelve Black Gnat. When T. C. saw the danger of losing this fish, he nobly jumped into the icy water to his armpits and barged down the current to the other side of the river to net her out on that side. I shall always remember this act of spontaneous sportsmanship and be grateful to him for it. Completely wet through but triumphant, he barged back again the way he had gone, with the fish held aloft. What a pal!

That the Apron became an angling shrine, a place to worship, was surely natural enough. I liked to sit by the pool.

From it there was an upstream view of broken water hurrying by leaning tree and drooping willow. Beyond, high white pumice cliffs changed their picture in varying lights; sometimes they were just cliffs and at others carried the illusion of distant Spanish castles. From there also the house perched on the opposite bank could be seen, and it was usual to get an encouraging wave from the veranda.

It was at the Apron Pool one summer evening that a swift grey bird flew past me with arrogance in his wing-beat. He was close to me, but did not vary his speed or direction a whit. He was a rare bird, even then. The time was noted as six o'clock; and every night for almost two weeks he followed the same purposeful course. Each night he kept the same beeline, and each time he merely glanced fearlessly at the man who waited there specially to see him pass.

Where had he been all day? Where was he going? He was well worth waiting for. It was a thrill to see his clear-cut wings, his streamlined shape and tail; his almost square head and flat whitish cheeks, the large watchful eye. Strength of purpose — fearless, aggressive, direct — was in every line of him. It was easy to see why the falcon is so much used in heraldry.

About the fifteenth evening I waited in vain, waited till darkness fell over the river, but no falcon came. He was seen no more, and was sadly missed.

Possibly his fearlessness had cost him dearly. It has wiped

his species almost from the face of the earth. The falcon, cursed as the chicken hawk, has few friends. In years this one was the only specimen seen there, and is therefore associated in my mind, for all time, with the Apron Pool.

For all these reasons the local anglers came to link me with the Apron. Though they knew my name for it, they preferred theirs: Kelly's Pool.

One fine summer night, as my wife and I were walking back to the house, the glint of a campfire caught my eye. Truda continued her way, but I turned back downstream to see what the fire signified, as we were in the middle of the fire season, a period of peril to both forest and farmland.

On a clear sandy beach below a large weeping willow, a very small and safe fire was burning. There was a glitter of glass in the firelight. A voice called, "Here he is!"

The speaker was sitting on a boulder, three quart-size beer bottles, two empty, by his side. His mate returned. I knew both these men slightly, one as a fisherman, who said, "Good day, Mr Kelly. We were looking for you."

"Good day," I replied, though it was after ten o'clock. "What did you want me for?"

"Oh, we just wanted a yarn. You see, I've been reading your fishing articles in the papers, and Charlie Loveridge, of National Park, agrees with me that you're wrong, y'know, you're wrong."

"About what?"

"'Bout bait casters. You don't like 'em an' reckon they spoil the fly fishing. Oh, I read everything you write as 'Tangataroa'. I know who you are. We want you to keep on writing, but all the same you're wrong, y'know, you're wrong. Call us hardware hurlers. But we catch the bloody cannibals, those big fish you fellers never see. Twelve-pounder caught here by Bill Bogue the other night. Only bloody cannibals! So we help you blokes and you can't see it."

There was no heat in this slightly belched tirade, and I had to agree that those big non-risers were cannibals and were

Waikato River – Broadlands

Trout fishing, Lake Okataina, Rotorua

harmful; but, all the same, on purely fly water a bait-caster was a nuisance, especially as he came slashing down a reach up which a dry-fly man was fishing.

There was no heat in my reply either — nor very much conviction.

"What are you here for, boys, if you are not fishing?"

"Oh, we're waiting for a ride."

"Ride! Is someone coming for you?"

"Yes. Bill in his bulldozer."

"Bulldozer?"

"Yes. He gives us a ride to home."

"But it's only two miles to walk!"

"Too bloody far. We'll wait for Bill."

"How fast does his machine go?"

"'Bout four miles an hour."

"Hope you've saved him a drink."

"Too right! Good old Bill."

As I bade the good old soldier and his fine Maori mate a pleasant journey home, the words followed me:

"You're wrong y'know. You're wrong. But keep on writing those articles. We all read 'em up in the bush, 'n we promise we won't bugger up your hole."

I'm glad to record that they did not "bugger up me hole".

E

12. "What's the Difference?"

We descended the winding road through the Rotoma Scenic Reserve on our return from Whakatane to Taupo. The high banks on our right and the deep gullies on our left were astonishingly rich in the greenery of native fern, konini (fuchsia), wineberry, fivefinger, mahoe, as well as taller specimens of second-growth trees. When the last of the innumerable corners was turned we saw Lake Rotoma shining in the evening light below us through the final cutting. It was just one more agreeable view in a hundred miles of agreeable views.

The sight of a sheet of water like Rotoma means much to many people; to the angler it means trout.

I heard myself saying, "I've only fished that lake once, many short years ago."

Why did I blurt this out? The driver, I knew, had caught a fish, but only one or two on a spoon once.

"What was it like?" my friend asked politely.

"Oh, pretty dull," I replied. "It was only trolling a fly behind a dinghy."

"You'd sooner fish a dry fly, perhaps?"

"Yes, of course. It's wonderful, when you can get it."

"What's the difference between wet and dry? Don't you let the dry touch the water?"

"Yes, we do; but the fly is specially dressed and oiled to make it float on the surface where the trout take it for a real insect floating down the current."

"I see."

"Yes. You actually see the fish rise and take your fly in his mouth. You must time the strike correctly or you will miss him. It's most exciting."

"Well then," he asked, "what do you do with a wet fly?"

The car slowed down as we drove through the silent glory of Hongi's Track and passed the Wishing Tree. After this there was only about sixty miles to go so I knew I would have to be brief. At the end, or near the end, of my discourse, he pleased me immensely by commenting:

"So, in your two ways of fishing, it is a matter of whether your fly is *on* the water or *in* the water?"

"Yes. That's it in a nutshell."

By this time the lights of Taupo were coming into view, twinkling in their varied colours in the sharp frosty air. The thoughts of our blazing fire of matai logs and a roast dinner took over from the fishing, wet or dry.

If it had not been that my friend seemed to speed up towards the end of our trip, I could have given him an instance of how the dry fly can bring success where any other would have been quite useless; but there wasn't time.

The scene of this story was a wide stony reach on one of the branches of the Whakapapa. At this point the current took a slight turn away from our bank and fell over a shallow shelf. Here and there larger boulders were scattered through the small stones.

My companion was Douglas Hall, then Mayor of Taumarunui, who, as a South Islander in his younger days, had learned the art of dry-fly fishing. We had both done fairly well and were on our way to a good pool farther up the river. He was leading the way. Suddenly he stopped and called back:

"Greg, look at that fish in the little pool by the boulder."

He dropped to one knee and started false casting. It was not till his fly dropped that I saw the fish. It was a big brownie in less than a foot of water. His pool, lying between two low boulders, measured about three feet long by two feet wide. He was steadily feeding on some form of insect drifting into and over his little bay.

Three times, with absolute accuracy, the dry fly, I think a Kakahi Queen, his usual favourite, came down ahead of the pool and floated unheeded over the fish.

"No good. I'll try something else."

I do not know what he tied on though I noticed he did not hurry as he calmly oiled the new fly and went through the same procedure. Again the fly did everything required. Again, on several trips, it was ignored.

"Damn," the angler muttered, as he wound in to remove that fly and tie on his third offer, which was, I'm sure, a Red-tipped Governor about size ten.

All this time the fish kept on feeding steadily, swinging from side to side; and all that time Hall remained in his kneeling position on the stones.

The third fly was tied on with steady fingers and un-hurriedly, in spite of the high excitement he could not help feeling. Again he oiled up and, when ready, he started to work out his line to the correct length in the approved way before allowing the fly to drop on the same spot as before. This time, as the fly came over him the fish lunged at it greedily, was hooked and, after the usual tussling brown-trout flurry, was brought to the edge where I netted it.

The point of this story, as I said before, is to illustrate the value of the dry-fly method where no other system, known to me anyway, could possibly have succeeded.

And, as a demonstration of angling skill, I still consider that one the most convincing and delightful.

It will be seen that this sort of fishing calls for several essentials. Upstream casting is one, for the simple reason that the fish, with head upstream, can be more *closely* approached from behind; and as it is watching for food being borne down by the current – not necessarily on the top – its movements can be more clearly detected.

By crouching, or kneeling, as in the above instance, the angler is less likely to be seen in his final approach.

The shorter the free line the shorter the casting, so the accurate placing of the fly on the water is made easier. In addition, there is less line likely to fall behind the fish because there is less line in action.

The skill of being able to judge the length of the cast or "throw" so that the fly touches down *lightly* a few feet upstream ahead of the fish, and in such a way that the cast "gut" does not fall across or too near the fish and scare him, is what really counts in this game. It has been my experience that the development of this degree of skill with a rod is not as difficult as it may appear to be, or as many angling writers have made it out to be. Like learning to play a fiddle, it takes determined practice. It is far simpler to master, but, unlike the fiddle, gets on no one's nerves except those of the learner himself. One good first step is to be able to kill the energy of the cast four or so feet above the water at the same instant that the living line from the left hand eases out the "shoot". The effect is twofold. The energy which the arm transmitted to the line is all absorbed in the air above the water and, instead of the line slapping down on the water, which is, of course, fatal, it falls of its own weight, and the fly settles on the water rather than falling into it.

When an angler can see a feeding fish and has a go at him in this way, he can soon learn whether he has done his work properly or not. The fish will advise him on this point.

One more essential: the dry, or floating, fly has to be watched. Otherwise a fish can take it and spit it out without the angler knowing anything about it. And then there is the critical period between the moment the fish is seen to take the fly and the angler sets the hook. This can be a matter of a full second to two or even three seconds.

It will be obvious that this rough description is not all that's in this particular form of angling. A considerable amount of knowledge of the flies for the river, the judging of the speed of the current, the angle of sun-rays, and how to cast against the wind are important.

For all this, nobody should be afraid to use a dry fly. It's not dead easy, but it is really no mystery. Possibly one of its benefits to the angler is that it's good for his soul.

Turning to the other style of fishing – wet fly. It is no great task to learn the rudiments. It is more of a "chuck-and-chance-it" game and the fish virtually hook themselves. Perhaps its greatest advantage is the wide availability. One can cast a wet fly in a running stream and the current washes it down to the limit of free line when it sweeps across in a curve to a point straight below the rod. The angler then starts to retrieve his line in whatever manner and at whatever pace he finds effective.

There must always be some contact or tension between rod and fly so that, when the fly is taken, the angler feels the pull and strikes the hook home.

Simple as this sounds, it is full of essential "dodges" most of which can only be learned by fishing.

Unless restricted to the use of a single fly, as at Taupo and Rotorua, the wet-fly user can tie on two or even three flies at different points along his cast, thus giving the fish a sort of à la carte menu to choose from. This technique probably resulted in the hoary joke about the angry fisherman who, after fishless casting of many patterns, finally threw his fly book in the stream with a profane invitation to the fish to make their own selection.

The use of wool and feathers tied to a hook to "lure fish to their destruction" is traced back to the second century. Hence we learn that wet-fly fishing is a much more venerable craft than its stiff-necked rival whose rise to power is of comparatively recent date.

Most anglers use the wet fly to begin with. A small proportion of these develop into dry-fly anglers. Some men in this group fish happily wet or dry just as it suits them. Others who graduate from the wet to the dry scorn the former method as crude, and on a day that is unsuitable for the dry fly because of water stain or weather, prefer to go home empty handed rather than "grope" downstream with a sunken fly.

It is very interesting to probe into the reasons why this "higher art" persists in New Zealand. There is no private fishing here as in England, where a small group of club men rent a length of water, and where each member pays an equal share of the costs. They then draw up a set of rules governing the methods to be used, thus forming a code of ethics. How strict these rules are was told last week in a Taupo tackle shop by a member of such a club. This gentleman had called for a short-term licence and some items of tackle including, of course, the patterns of local flies. In reply to the question as to where he should go to fish the dealer suggested Waitahanui, then fishing well. When he reached the door of the shop, the visitor turned and asked.

"What sized trout might one expect heah?"

"Oh," said the dealer, "You should catch round about three- or five-pounders."

The visitor raised his chin and stared bleakly at the shopman for a moment before stepping out of the door in silence.

Later in the day he was back, acting like an excited and delighted schoolboy and talking in italics. Out of it all the dealer gleaned the information that his visitor had caught two fish, one five and a half and the other a six-pounder.

Before he left the shop he related his experiences in England. "I belong to a fishing club. There are just a few of us. We rent a length of trout water. When we reach our beat, we draw lots as to position – who should start at the top of the water and who should be at the lowest. Given a fair time for each man to get to his place, a little bell is rung and you start fishing. When the man who started at the top reaches the bottom he may return to his old position again. By that time all have fished over the water once. Then we may go through again in the same order."

"What does the fishing cost you?"

"We pay the owner a thousand a year," was the answer.

"And," he added, "the record fish in the club, so far, is a one-and-three-quarter pounder."

A Taupo licence is three pounds ten shillings for the whole year's fishing, and we are not confined to three-quarters of a mile of river bank.

As yet, there is no organized club of dry-fly purists in New Zealand. Nevertheless there are qualifiers for the title of purist to be met with on almost any river where the dry is practical.

Such a one was T. C. with whom I had spent a number of happy days on the Whakapapa when we used nothing else. Then a series of incidents occurred which demonstrate the kind of purism I mean.

I had been camped for a week on the banks of the Whakapapa and five days of first class sport had been my share. When T. C. called to have another day with me it was natural, therefore, that I should urge my companion to fish the choice spots ahead of me while I just tagged along, enjoying his company, listening to his conversation and watching his efforts. In spite of his faultless casting with flies known to be effective on that water, it was disappointing that not a fish put up his neb in two hours, over nearly a mile of beautiful water. Several patterns of flies were used; all appeared to touch down correctly and be lifted before any "drag" could take place.

My own efforts in the lesser pools got no response either, but this did not worry me. My desire was that T. C. catch a fish. His industry and skill deserved it.

Then we came to the Rainbow Pool which was large and deep against a curving flood-cut bank. The current ran from our right into this pool over a shelf of stones. The "eye" of the pool rarely failed to produce a fish. It was no go! My friend, by now feeling a bit glum, burst out, "No good, Greg. No fish here." He started to move away to the next pool upstream.

Fortunately, the bend of the river took him to the right away from the field of the trout's vision.

"Wait a tick, T.C. I'd like to try this pool."

"You'll be wasting time."

What's time to a sitting hen, I thought.

I had tied on a Purple Jessie nymph which I slipped right up just below the lip of stone above the "eye" and as the fly came back, a foot or so deep, there was a flash under water. I struck instantly and had a fish to deal with. My irrepressible yell brought T.C. to a halt and he turned in astonishment.

"What! You've got one?"

The line went slack.

"I had one."

Not waiting a minute I cast up again. Another flash and a quick strike with the rod. This time the hook held. "Luck of a Chinaman! Luck of a Chinaman!" T.C. kept saying, half in excitement and half in anger; but he netted out my fish, which turned out to be a three-and-a-half pound hen brownie.

"Both those fish were hooked, T.C., because they were feeding on nymphs. It's useless offering them floaters. Why not try one of mine?"

"No. That's *wet-fly* fishing."

"Be reasonable, T.C.," I pleaded. "Members of the Fly Fishers' Club in London now use these minor tactics as advocated by one of its members, G. E. M. Skues. It's quite accepted."

"It's wet-fly fishing all the same." And he marched off.

I went back to where I had stood before, and again the nymph dived into the deep. Incredibly, another red blur was seen with the result that a fine three-and-three-quarter pound rainbow got the shock of her young life.

T.C. had just reached the next bend when my yell

arrested him. I hoped that now he would be convinced, but he merely shook his fist at me.

When my new fish was in the net I looked up to see my friend changing his fly again, and thought that at last he had seen the light. Not a bit of it. He had merely put on another dry fly and, sad to relate, fished out the day without seeing any fish other that the two victims of the minor tactics in my bag.

Here was a New Zealander who must have delighted the shade of the great F. M. Halford, the High Priest of Purism!

13. *A Lesson Without Words*

Now here's a warning word for you:
When you angle for a trout or two
Keep in mind, whate'er you do
That brilliant sunbeams angle too.

In my camping days by the Whakapapa I had arranged with a Taumarunui friend that we would have a day on the river together. I was pleased to have his company as, for one thing, he knew the water well. He was also an enthusiastic dry-flier.

Long before, I had learned on the Pareora that a bumble-footed approach to fishing water was fatal to success and that it paid to be cautious, but I was still making a mistake of which I had too long been unaware.

This is the record of how this fault was corrected without a single word being said about it.

When Alex and I met it was about ten in the morning. The air was bright and warm and the water in first-class order. My friend led the way to an attractive pool, but instead of fishing it, he waded straight in and invited me to join arms to get across. Though the water was fairly deep and swift, we had no trouble, as he knew exactly what to do.

Again he surprised me for, instead of fishing the pool from that bank, he moved on to a clear, well-used track through the bush and followed it for about half a mile down to where this branch of the Whakapapa joined the Wanganui.

Again he crossed the smaller stream to the western bank and stood at the bottom of an attractive pool.

"This we call Rainbow Pool because one of our party can nearly always pick one out of it. Take whichever half you like, Greg, but the lower half must be fished first."

I elected to try the lower and started casting. Nothing rose to my Cochy by the time I had reached the half-way bush. Alex also covered the same water on the way to his stretch, using a wingless Red-tipped Governor – his favourite – but nothing showed up until he had covered almost all the water, then a lovely four-pounder accepted him.

"Here he is, Greg." I did not need to be told for his reel became loudly vocal as the fish plunged down towards the Wanganui. I belted the water with my open net and he rushed up again where Alex played him out.

My friend's next move was up by way of a narrow thorny opening to the pool above, and in tough going, he continued up along that bank. As we went, I noticed some pretty good water where progress and casting would have been simpler from and along the opposite bank. Luckily I did not ask him why he had not fished that side going down the other way. This would have disclosed my ignorance.

As we fished along to where we had planned to have lunch, I noticed he always scanned the sky before going too close to the pool. What he was working out was the angle of the sun's rays on the water.

By lunch time I had the satisfaction of seeing him hook two more fish. Though I had none, this did not worry me. I was far more interested in watching this man's careful tactics than in my own effort.

After his return to Taumarunui I attended to camp chores and prepared cooking details for my evening meal. After this I rested till three o'clock.

Not being game enough to cross the rapid water alone where we had crossed in the morning, I retraced my way down the western bank, crossed the shallows below the Rainbow and returned up the eastern bank to tackle the pools I thought we ought to have fished in the morning. Some old boot marks pointed downstream, indicating that someone else had fished them with wet fly. The result of my efforts were two good fish; one slab and two other small ones liberated. "So," I thought, "these pools are as good as they look." And still I had not taken the hint.

A week later Alex was back again, this time with two mates. These two struck straight up the river on the western bank. Alex and I went down going through the exact performance we did before. I think we had a fish each by lunch time. The others also had success. My only record is for the whole bag for the party – twelve fish.

Lunch was a go-easy affair, because the Whakapapa is a boulder-strewn river, very tiring and difficult. At last we got to work again and it was agreed that Alex and I would fish the upper sections while our friends went down to the Rainbow to fish back.

Waiting for guidance and eager to learn from these men who knew the river, I was the last to move. Without the slightest hesitation, as though this was the regular thing to do, they all trooped across the log bridge to the eastern bank. Light dawned at last on my dimness and I realised that great importance was attached by these expert dry-fly men to the angle of the sun's rays.

In our subsequent forgatherings the procedure was always the same: in the morning the casting was done from the western bank; in the afternoon it was from the eastern. It was as simple as falling backwards in the river.

Fish take more notice of a shadow than they do of a movement on the bank. I remember once watching a feeding fish when I was taking notes on the bird life along the river. Although I was close behind him, he did not seem to notice me. It was good fun watching his industrious hunting from side to side. Suddenly a blackbird flew across the river throwing his shadow on the water. The fish vanished.

14. The Seductive Nymph

Glorious sport can be enjoyed by using a wet fly upstream. The value of this system should have occurred to me years before it did.

When T. C. jumped into the Apron Pool to save me from losing a good fish, I knew very well that the Black Gnat fly, though cast as a dry fly, had sunk and been taken by that fish well below the surface; and this was not an isolated experience.

In his *Minor Tactics of the Chalk Stream* G. E. M. Skues, of the Fly Fishers' Club (London) had revealed his system in 1910; but it seems I must have thought it applied only to the chalk stream.

The fly which Basil Humphrey developed and called the Twilight Beauty really does resemble an ephemeral form which hatches on the Whakapapa generally between four p.m. and dusk. I had fished these rises from time to time, and had been quite proud of myself if my fly had been accepted. Many times, of course, there was complete and dismal failure.

On one of these occasions the insects were dimpling the calmer water well below the big rock at the head of the pool. They were breaking out of their wing cases and sailing down the rather fast current as they fluttered and stretched their wings. Scores and scores of these would fly off the water and stagger upstream. Not a single fish broke the surface to interfere with them. I put my Twilight Beauty on the water and it looked exactly like the natural, but nothing happened to it either.

After many attempts with it, I tried other patterns one after the other, perhaps six in all, without the slightest notice being taken of them by the trout I knew perfectly well were there.

I moved forwards a few yards and in less turbulent water could see two trout slashing and darting excitedly first one way and then another. They were quite three feet down. It was amazing they did not see me, I was so close above them. Moving back slowly I put on a size ten Red-tipped Governor and placed that over them again and again. It was useless. Still the enormous hatch went on, flies galore rising in the air and being snapped up in dozens by fantails.

In complete frustration I took the fly off the water, and instead of the false casting to dry it, I tore the wings off it and as much of the hackle as I could with finger- and thumb-nail. The result of this treatment left only a thick knot of hackle and a herl body with its red-tipped tail. Wetting the wretched thing with saliva I chucked it up to the head of the pool where it plopped into the water and sank out of sight at once. The cast was visible as it floated back. When I saw it twitch a little, I struck instantly and was into a solid fish which turned the scales at five pounds! Incredibly, two more fish followed in quick succession in the same way. Then the hatch was over. An examination of the stomach contents showed nothing else but the nymphal form of the hatch fly.

Clearly these fish were intercepting the hatching form soon after it had left the bottom of the river and were not at all interested when it reached the surface.

Here without question were Skues's chalk-stream tactics shown to be the answer to such fish as these feeding beneath the surface.

One more point; the nymphs the chalk-stream man used were dressed to imitate *exactly* the sub-imago of the hatching fly. I have found that it does not matter at all about exact imitation, so long as the size and general appearance are much the same as the nymph they are hunting. My raped

Red-tipped Governor was as rough as bags. So, too, are many nymphs themselves as they leave the bottom. A lot of them found in the gut had not quite kicked themselves free from the caddis cases which are made of sticks and stones.

The important thing in this sort of work is to be able to see the floating cast. When it does anything unusual the rod must be whipped upward instantly. In my own case I am aware of missing many fish that should have been hit simply because I had not twigged the sign soon enough.

When light – or eyesight – is inferior and the cast cannot be detected, there is another trick worth trying which, though known now to many anglers, was one of my own. It was for fun that I used it first.

On one of the smaller braids of the Whakapapa I noticed a fair-sized trout feeding busily below a ripple and put a Cochy over him. He twice followed the floater down the pool a yard or so but made no effort to take it, simply returning to his original position to go on with his feeding.

Instead of putting another fly on the cast I picked a nymph out of my hat, tied a foot length of gut to the Cochy and bent the nymph on this extra bit of gut. My idea was that I could watch what happened, if anything, by the action of the Cochy. Both flies hit the rocks above the ripple and I could see the big Cochy bobbling down the current, but the nymph was below the surface and out of my sight. Suddenly the Cochy disappeared and I struck smartly, hooking the fish, a brownie of two pounds, securely.

Now this experiment led me to think I had something so good that for ever more I could catch trout when I wanted to. Lo, human vanity was never more misplaced. Certainty in any style of catching trout just does not exist, though this system has saved the day for me many times.

At or about that time the New Zealand *Sportsman* was using some of my fishing articles, so I sent them this one. It had a quite unexpected result. One day when I visited Morrie MacKenzie's editorial office he said: "Mr Webber

John Sierpinski with a fine brook trout

Waimarino River, deep in the North Island bush

would like to meet you." So it came to pass that E.G.W. and I met for the first time; immediately the subject was fishing.

"My chief compositor came in the other day and showed me the set-up of that yarn of yours about using a sinking fly below a floating one. I've never heard of that wheeze. Sounds interesting."

"He a keen fisherman too?"

"Oh, yes. Quite."

I hardly believed Webber. How could two keen anglers work in the same office and get their paper out on time?

That was the beginning of my having to put up with Webber. He at once started to bully me into writing a book. It served him right that he had, in the finish, to do most of the work himself.

May I add I wrote this one unbeknown to him.

F

15. The Snaky Cast

During the war, when transport was awkward, a Taumarunui angler was kind enough to drive me down to the river. He knew the water well, but had somehow concluded that I had never fished it. I let the moment slip by when I should have told him of previous visits. Afterwards it was too late.

The pools he put me on to were the best ones on the whole mile of river we fished that day and he took the poorer ones for himself, which was a token of his natural sportsmanship. But he was severe on my casting.

"You're a bugger of a fisherman, Kelly. Your line falls on the water like a dog's breakfast."

I had to admit it. At any rate, when we came to the end of our fishing, I had two jolly good fish, a rainbow and a brown, and he had three rainbows all around three pounds each. In comparing notes it turned out that I had raised twice the number of fish that had responded to his superior efforts in casting, but he was not impressed with these statistics. "No accounting for tastes," he commented dryly.

He had no idea of the surgical ordeal I had been through which had cost me the total use of my right arm for a year.

His rude but well-meant remarks caused me to make up my mind to put in all the time possible practising upstream casting. Though no dabster, even to this day, my casting did improve enough to escape a scolding when we next met.

One thing emerged from this experience: The better and straighter my casting became, the fewer fish rose to my dry fly.

Occasionally I noticed a "badly" cast fly with a snaky line

on the water rose a fish. Sometimes these rotten shots resulted in catching one.

The upshot of all this sort of thing was a deliberate effort to put the line down on the water so that it looked like a New Zealand road does from the air. In other words, a snaky cast. Now in dry-fly fishing I always endeavour to make a "dog's breakfast" of my cast, because experience has shown that the fish don't mind. In fact they seem to like the snaky cast, and when we come to think about it, there is a fair enough explanation for it.

The earliest dabblers in the art of angling with a surface floating fly, upstream, must soon have realised that fish never touched it when it was being pulled or otherwise interfered with by the cast or line. This they called "the drag", a term that has come down to us and which we still use.

The whole essence of dry-fly work is that the fly deceives the trout into accepting it as a real bug, spider, or fly. This can only happen when the fly acts like the genuine article.

It stands to reason that a floater is not acting naturally when it is being pulled along or towed like a girl on water skis.

Trout are silly in many ways, but they are not complete imbeciles.

There is no way to prevent drag. All that can be done is to delay it; and this is where, in my opinion, the snaky cast is worth something. It allows the fly to float down several feet farther than is possible with a straight, expertly laid line. I can still feel envy when watching experts for their quite extraordinary skill in putting a lure far out and as straight as a rifle shot. Even before the surgeons cut through useful bone and muscle I could never approach such skill; but catching trout is not always managed by the mere use of a rod. Furtunately the lovely sport needs a good deal more than bone and muscle. My semi-useless arm gave me my snaky cast which postponed the fatal drag.

Clearly the drag is troublesome only to the dry-fly angler.

It does not matter in wet-fly work or in nymph fishing. In fact the only way to use a down-the-current wet fly is to employ drag in various ways to coax the fish to grab it as a living thing.

Experts sometimes delay drag by a trick called "mending the cast". This is simple enough and is used when a quick current is running between the fly and the rod. The downstream belly in the line is lifted with a quick flick and tossed upstream again like a loop in a skipping rope. My own experiments with this system have not brought me much fortune.

It is unnecessary to say that the fly itself is all that is seen by the trout. Curlicues ahead of the fly or anywhere near it will scare the daylights out of the trout and put him down. Another thing to remember is that the snaky throw must be reasonable and make just enough wiggles in the line so the current in straightening these out allows the fly that little extra freedom to float without drag. A few feet or even inches can make all the difference.

Note: John Alden Knight in his *The Modern Angler* (Chas. Scribner, NY, 1936) makes a big feature of the value of the loose wavy cast in upstream casting, wet or dry.

16. There's Many a Slip . . .

It had been a dour afternoon when the fish did not appear to be interested in anything, not even naturals, and I had just about given up by the time I reached the shallow ford that crossed the second branch of the Whakapapa.

Ahead of me was a well-known bank upon which a crop of garden mint was growing to a height of four feet. The river was very wide at this point – for which reason it had been chosen for the ford – but it was deep against the mint bank. Along this I was casting a Purple Jessie from just above the ford when a horseman came cantering through the bush. If he had continued every fish in the pool would have scattered; but with a natural courtesy the young Maori waited for my signal to come on. This gave me time to move up to the top end of the reach. Almost at the very top a rainbow rose and was hooked. The horseman dismounted and ran forward in excitement.

"By Jo, it's beauty fish!"

Certainly there was plenty of action and I felt sure of landing him if he could be kept above me. However the fish had other ideas and broke downstream leaping. He splashed across the ford before I could do a thing to stop him. Now I was in trouble, as below the ford the stream broke into rapids at the bottom of which it turned sharply left. It was impossible for me to follow as the far bank was covered with tangled bush, and the near side with big boulders laced with blackberry and lupins – those evil partners of the river-bed. I held on and let him run and then —

"He's gone, Marty."

"Did you loss him, ehoa?" he called with a wail.

"Yes, Marty. I loss him all right."

"By Jo, that's tep bad luck, ehoa. He was beauty fish."

I wound up my line to find that the fish had only borrowed my fly for the time being. He gave it back uninjured.

This was an understandable loss of a fish. But what about dozens of other fish lost without reasonable explanation?

On the opening morning of 1950 I hooked a rainbow of delightful action which leapt and leapt often enough, one would have thought, to knock himself out. His idea was to get rid of the nasty burr in his lip and who could blame him for that? He looked to be a good five-pounder, and so might have proved had the size twelve Purple Jessie not come away. Surely after having held for his early convulsions, it should have stuck the battle out. It just got tired and let go.

Five fish got rid of me in exactly, or almost exactly, the same way out of seven hooked on the dry fly that morning. As far as could be judged on the other eight days I was able to spend on the river during that period of leave, I landed only nine fish out of twenty-two hooked. Six others were liberated.

One of the evenings is remembered as a most galling one. The evening was mild and calm so I asked my wife and her friend, Miss Robb, to come along and see how things were done. They chattered happily about the glory of the sunset and the bands of golden light that glowed along the indented horizon, whilst I was working with the Purple Jessie, a fly over which the trout seemed to go mad early in the season. A large rainbow jumped at the fly, missed it, then chased it, slashing it below with him as I hit him firmly. Here surely was a soundly hooked fish. I had him on for quite a while and got several jumps out of him as he tore up the pool and down again. Steadily he was drawn with (I'll swear it) the greatest care towards the still water at the lower end of the pool. The fly came free, and he sank slowly from my sight without even a kick from his tail.

Of course this sort of thing happens to us all. It is nothing. But for it to happen four times with the only four fish hooked, the last one actually on its side near the edge, yet lost, was more than angling blood could bear.

I hope I rarely play the part of a bad loser. I did that night.

There were fish which gave me no chance. For instance, just fifty yards above a stiff waterfall my Claret Jessie floated nicely down a broad wavy current till it almost passed me, when a twist in the ripple submerged the fly. As I started to lift the line there was a crescent hump in the water as a good fish grabbed the fly. I hooked him firmly as though wet-fly fishing.

How good it was to feel that solid fellow if only for a few seconds. He turned his head downstream and left for "home and mother" so I had no chance unless he could be turned upstream again. If he could reach the fall he would certainly be lost, so all that could be done was to increase the pressure on the line more and more by squeezing the line between finger and thumb. It was no good. The fly came away and the comedy ended with the fly bouncing back merrily and mockingly.

I should have liked to have seen that fish. One might as well have been hooked to the back of a bus.

The peculiar part of this experience was the slow pace he set. One could call it a steady march; quite unlike the usual reel-squealing run of either a brown or a rainbow. But at any rate, here was a fish that gave the angler no chance whatever of landing it. Its loss was no puzzle. If one could have chased him along the bank – the water was too deep to wade – he might have been beaten in the pools below the fall. So his escape was not a matter for grief or anger. Quite unlike the four mentioned above.

A severe chill kept me a prisoner at the cottage for day after day while the splendid fishing water of the Whakapapa sparkled and gurgled down below. I had to sit on the veranda and look at that half-mile length of river and at the green ranges beyond, where glades of kowhai were breaking gold above willows in new leaf along the banks of the Wanganui, until almost the end of my leave.

On my last evening I determined to make an effort to get a fish or two to take home to Wellington, and went to a fine spot on the Wanganui. This was a long reach below a high cliff where much success had been mine over the years. It held one terrible menace. This was an enormous rock fifteen or twenty feet from the far bank with fairly fast water running between it and the bank. A fish which ran down that little rip would break the cast on the rock.

As I sat watching the water, what appeared to be a big grasshopper flew over the pool, bashed against the bank and fell in the water, downstream from the rock. He floated down quite a distance kicking feebly, then there came a mighty smash on the surface and he was no more. Somewhat excitedly I sneaked down through the bushes and gained the water below the "rise" and put up a big size eight Cochy well upstream. It took much the same course as the hopper and, on that very first trip, was grabbed by a rainbow. The brute tore straight upstream towards that evil rock, and I had to give him the butt to keep him away from it. Credit goes to the size eight hook, for it held. He turned downstream again and I landed him a hundred yards farther down on a sandy beach: four and three-quarter pounds.

I left the pool at once with the idea of getting to the cottage before dark. On the way I passed a loggy pool where the stream raced between a ridge of stones and a pile of flood timbers. It looked a hopeless place from which to draw a fish. As I came towards it I saw a brown trout steadily feeding. As it was getting late I tied on a Twilight – also size eight – and he accepted it like a dove and was unceremoniously bustled out of the dangerous water to where the stream broadened out and shallowed. There he put up a good show, but the fly held and the net claimed his nearly three pounds. Those were the only two fish out of thirty-nine hooked to be landed consecutively. Was this due to the use of size eight hooks? It is easy to conclude that it was. "The bigger the hook, the deeper the bite" we might agree. There is another side to this question: small flies attract more trout than do big flies.

We must also keep in mind that a very light rod, say five and three-quarter ounces, just has not got the "snap" to pull a big hook into a fish as efficiently as it can a small hook, for which it was constructed. This applies even in wet-fly fishing downstream when the trout, as often as not, hooks himself — something he cannot do in upstream casting, when the angler has to do the hitting. It has been my experience, so far, that my nine foot Farlow of six ounces is not reliable to drive a size four wet fly into the jaw of a fish, that is an adult fish, unless I lower the point and give the line a good tug with my fingers. If the hook is caught in the tongue or gullet, that is different; one rarely loses these.

At this moment I'm burning with indignation after losing two fine rainbows on two different nights when fishing at Jellicoe Point in the Waipehi. Both fish gave displays, the former was clear of the water in three separate leaps and the latter twice. Both freed themselves and sent the fly back to me. It is a very handsome fly of red setter pattern. Now on Friday morning (this sounds like a Webber story) I took the fly to examine it, thinking the point might be blunt or something. It had no barb on the hook and had never had a barb, just the merest snick with the tool that cuts the shank to make the barb. Now that's bad enough, but the salt was rubbed into my wounds by my friend Ken yesterday. He rang me about another business altogether and before he could tell me what it was, I started to chant my losses and my woes but hadn't got far when he cut in. "Oh, you got some of those flies! So did I. Same pattern. No barb on any of 'em." And he added — I could almost hear his Heilan' blood bubble — "The fellow charged me two shillings each for them. I could'a got the same patterns from ——'s shop for one and three. And *they* would 'a had barrbs." I almost forgot to ask him what he'd rung up about.

Surely hook maker, fly dresser, or dealer should have spotted the fault in these hooks. Or did they?

It's twenty miles from my home to Jellicoe Point, eighty for the only two fish hooked. Ken and I have resolved to examine the hook of each fly for future use.

We realise that from the moment any trout is hooked there is a fair possibility of its being lost. So should it be. The sure thing, in any sport, soon loses its flavour.

We might use unbreakable gut or nylon, and flies with double hooks, to be more sure of getting our fish, but what fun would that be for anyone except a pot-hunter?

Our losses should be reasonable and our kills moderate for the full enjoyment of angling.

17. Flash Floods

From its birthplace in the Whakapapa Glacier on Mount Ruapehu to its junction with the Wanganui the splendid Whakapapa's life journey is a short one, rather less than forty miles.

The glacier is about a mile north of Crater Lake and some 7,000 feet above sea level and it is from this considerable height that the two branches of the Whakapapa start their rapid course. Both streams, one "iti" (small) and the other "nui" (big) come together above the Whakapapa Gorge to form the river.

Like all rivers this one has many tributaries along its course, but the bulk of its volume comes from the glacier.

From its home at 7,000 feet it drops to 2,000 feet at Raurimu (roughly half its length), and to 1,500 at Owhango Gorge. In its last five miles the river drops a further 600 feet before it joins the Wanganui. Nature has taken care of the terrible impetuosity of this river by throwing in its path mighty rocks and twisting gorges that break the strength of its flow and check its destructive power.

Nature's great wisdom has again steadied the wild waters by a build-up over the centuries of a delta through which the river braids for the last five miles of the valley.

The fishing pools are scattered along the two main branches and the various braids into which these branches are split. Though the fishing lengths are reasonably steady from the frightening cascades of the higher reaches, the angler fishing the Whakapapa for the first time can easily find himself in trouble because of the unexpected pace of the water. Long before I ever visited the Whakapapa I had been warned by an old pen-friend on fishing matters, Jack Worrall of Taumarunui, of the dangerous nature of this river and of the disconcerting trick it had of sending down flash floods.

These warnings were brought sharply to my mind one night when I was in my little tent below the log bridge. It was about eight o'clock and pitch dark when I heard loud male voices raised in excitement. I went along to see what was the cause of the shouting. An articulated logging truck was half-way over the bridge; water was flowing over the two logs of which the bridge was formed. Normally these were several feet above the river. I had crossed there dryshod about three hours before. All I could see was the dark mass of the truck and its load of logs, and a figure holding an oil hurricane lantern on the near end of the bridge.

Above the noise of the waters I heard the driver shouting angrily: "Keep still, you silly bastard, or I'll be in the drink in a minute."

Cold with fear I watched, realising that the only guide the driver had was the weak light of the lamp held by his mate. As there was no decking on the logs of the bridge, all the driver could do was to drive towards that light and hope his wheels rode the two flattened tree trunks. Gradually the enormous vehicle crawled forward yard by yard until the bank was reached. The bearer of the lantern got in beside his mate and the dark mass moved up the cutting on its way. Next time I visited the river the bridge had a decking of heavy planks.

One of these flash floods will be remembered by two old friends of mine from Auckland. I came upon them at the Apron Pool one late afternoon just as they had exhausted the possibilities of the pool without any tangible results. It was in the opening month of the season in weather conditions which had been unfavourable for several days. Suddenly all was well. The weather cleared up and after two hot sunny days the water became clear. After the usual greetings Mac said: "Isn't this your favourite pool?"

I acknowledged that it was, adding that, in my opinion, it was the second best reach on the river. Some time later came the canny question: "And which is the best pool?"

My reply was: "The one on the island there."

"Ever catch anything in it?"

"No. Not now. You see, I do not fish it any more."

"Best pool and you don't fish it! Why?"

"Because it has a hoodoo on it. Every time I've been there something unpleasant has happened to me, from being twice swept off my feet, in armpit waders – and once I only just got out – to the losing of my best book of flies, my finest fishing knife, and ripping my new thigh-boots on a submerged wire."

Mac turned to the Skipper. "Superstitious, you see. It's the Irish in him."

The old blue-water sailor did not quite second his friend's chaffing, but added gravely; "Do you mind if we try to break your hoodoo?"

I said I would be delighted and then left for the Wanganui river which is half a mile away through the totaras of the reserve.

Next morning their camp was a happy spot. In great glee they told me of their success at the hoodoo breaking. They had had a really wonderful evening. The Skipper had caught a six-pounder! It was splendid to see these confirmed Aucklanders really enjoy themselves in this delightful but then little known river valley. They had discovered the sort of pool that anglers dream about.

Now I do admit to having a soft spot for this pool in spite of its treatment of me. It was beautiful. It lay at the bottom of a long, broad reach where the water hurried down over fairly large stones and flattened out quietly to form the pool. From below, this white water of the reach looked like some patriarchal giant's beard. I had a habit, when passing along the track which ran along the top of a cut bank, of leaning my hand on a young totara to gaze upon it.

A fairly fast and deep rip had to be waded in order to get on to the island from which the pool was fished. So it was only possible to get there when the river was about normal, as it was at the time.

My friends returned to this pool the following night. The evening, following some hours of hot sun, was perfect for the dry fly. My wife came with me to Blackberry Bar, a good dry-fly water which also required wading over a small but swift gut of current to reach the stony bench from which to cast over the rising trout. One three-and-a-half pound rainbow rewarded me. I lost another and missed two more. A chilliness crept down on Wordsworth's "current of the water breeze", and it was for this reason we decided to return to the cottage. This swift gut was apparently unchanged as we recrossed it.

Ten minutes later we would have been trapped for the night on that cold, treeless ridge of stones for, as we crossed the log bridge, we saw that the water was rising like a wall. Such is the treachery of these mountain streams. We had forgotten the "snows on lower levels" of the weather man a few days before, and the effect of two blazing hot days.

The cottage was warm and welcoming; our supper was relished by a bright open fire of matai roots. The world outside was still, the sky pied with stars and clouds. What more could a humble fisherman desire for a holiday environment?

Built high on a pumice cliff which forms the real edge of the river valley the cottage looked down on the island and through the willows to the Hoodoo Pool. Lights moved on the island as we came out on the veranda to look at the night. It was eerie to see those mysterious lights flickering through the tangle of fern, willow and bramble. They seemed to be wandering aimlessly from place to place. What could they be? The mind groped for a human agency.

Maoris eeling, was one thought. But this was no good as it

was too early in the season. Then a fire was started, and by its glare a flash of a well-known head of white hair solved the problem. The enthusiasts of the morning had been trapped on that island for a miserable night when fishing the Hoodoo Pool. An attempt was made to reach them, but it had to be abandoned as the river was a raging torrent. No one's life was in danger.

Rain fell during the night, but by about four-thirty a.m., such is the odd temper of the Whakapapa, the water had fallen and two unlucky visitors ventured the crossing and managed it.

I saw their camp at midday. The porch was strewn with rods, waders, fishing gear. Wet clothing of all sorts festooned the wire fence. Silence reigned behind the closed door.

That night I heard their story. Fishing was good but when it was time to go back to their camp in the darkness, their fishing bags, left high above water level, were almost awash.

I heard no further references to the superstitions of my race. It was the wrong moment for me to speak even though I had to remember, furiously, a rather stern boyhood injunction never to say: "I told you so!"

18. Birds of the Riverside

There is always interest for the trout fisherman in watching birds. This has nothing whatever to do with the fact that the artificial flies he uses are made of their feathers. If an angler is observant some birds can be helpful to his sport. Fantails seen flying over a pool can tell him that a hatch of duns is in progress and that fish will be active there. Generally where birds are plentiful fish food is also present in the form of moths, beetles, cicadas or land grubs. When a lake fisherman sees no shags on the rocks he can feel pretty sure that fish are absent too. Apart from these considerations bird-watching has a charm for the man with eyes and ears to notice the antics and hear the notes of the little fellows.

Camped alongside a wild-life refuge of native forest I had many opportunities of enjoying the company of some not common birds. It was from my tent that I saw one morning, as the sun climbed up over the high ridge to light up my side of the river, two koekoea in flight together. It was the sight of a lifetime for me. This elusive migrant from Rarotonga, the long-tailed cuckoo of the pakeha, camouflages himself in the bush by lying along a branch. I once came upon him cleaning his beak on a mossy bough. Even his cry has the will-o'-the-wisp quality of a ventriloquist. Yet on this morning here were two flying from my camp towards the big cliff above the Wanganui, one behind the other, perhaps ten feet apart. Their long tails streamed out behind them; their directness, like a passenger plane, unmistakable.

Unlike his long-tailed namesake the shining cuckoo, of which there were scores in the valley, is not shy. Two were

The turbulent Tongariro: Bryan Atkinson in Waddell's Pool

Fishing the "Duchess" on the Tongariro River

Les Mark with a good "bag"

Les Mark landing a good fish
in the Wanganui River

sitting on the top wire of the fence, he and his wife. Their black backs and wings above their white barred throats and breasts gleamed like polished metal. He had just alighted holding in his beak a black, hairy grub which, with something of a swagger, he offered to his bride. The lass was not impressed. At the second offer she turned her head and looked away. Flying to her other side he renewed the offer, to be even more scornfully rejected as she again turned away. So he ate it himself. The pair sat side by side without a word or a sign for several minutes before she flew her undulating way over the river. He followed her.

Of course the little grey warbler, riro-riro, was there in numbers. As the wageless nurse of the cuckoo he just had to be. It is one of Nature's mysteries why the cuckoo builds no nest, hatches no egg, feeds no chick; but blithely passes all such plebian chores over to little dupes like this innocent creature only half its size.

Lovingly hatched, fed and cared for, the large cuckoo baby pushes out the warbler chicks and thrives on the industry of his foster parents whilst his real parents swagger around the countryside to be admired and listened for. The angler, listening to his sweet, weak, uncertain little song, which he never seems to complete properly, wonders if it is a sign, as alleged, of approaching rain.

There were paradise ducks along the river with little fear of and no respect for the angler. Start casting in the reach, and though a quarter of a mile upstream, a pair would be sure to fly down with their bugles blowing and flop right in the eye of the pool, thoroughly enjoying the mischief of completely spoiling one's sport.

Once I found a tiny grey duck alone in the wilderness. The wee thing swam rapidly across the current and down the water's edge on the other side. Later this little ball of yellow fluff repeated its anxious journey hundreds of yards farther down. No sign of mother or brother; his story was probably a tragic one.

G

There is an absorbing pleasure in trying to pick out the notes of the tui from those of the bell bird so closely akin in this place of harmony. Often there was kotare, the sacred kingfisher, counting on a tall whipstick high above the river. One, two, three; one, two, three. What? Children, minnows, blessings?

Every day the quail ran-and-paused, ran-and-paused, past my tent; the cock with his black banner held high in pride.

Down in the swampy parts between the rivers cock pheasants crowed at frequent intervals. Only the serpentine stoat could harm them there or that terrible enemy of feathered people, the domestic cat gone wild.

Little black and white tits sat on odd twigs trying to get over the hump about something; silver-eyes swarmed suddenly through mingimingi bushes in their endless search for food; those cheerful neighbours, the thrushes and black-birds, chattered about gardens, seeds and grubs.

Where the rivers join the wary grey duck rose in a small cloud to thrill the angler as they circled high to leave him the entire bend of the river junction for the half hour he might need it, always returning when he had moved on to another pool. Among the wild duck was a lone one of purely barnyard type. What harshness had driven her from the barnyard to such a lone spot? Was her choice permanent, or like the angler's of brief but happy duration?

Up the shining current, at no great height, the heavy black shags winged their way — hated fowl of the fisherman yet part of Nature's inscrutable scheme.

Fantails darted in among the bars of sunlight falling across the stream, their tiny beaks snipping like so many springs. A sucking noise with the lips would usually excite one to the tip of my outstretched rod. From there he would often flutter round my head. Should I fear for the Twilights in my old tweed hat? Back to the tip of the rod he would go, his weight not enough to bend it. There he would sway restlessly turning end for end half a dozen times. At the take-off the delicate tip bent and quivered. Snip, snip, and back again to the rod. What angler on the sacred chalk streams of Hampshire ever had a greater joy than this?

At night ruru broke the moonlit silence, creaking his first note before settling down to the soft "ru ru" that gave him his Maori name. His was a welcome note reminding me of many a past camp by mountain, lake and river.

For years I used to hear a strange wild cry of some bird that was not identified. Always the same single-toned note, harsh, like that of a large sea bird, it came from the high night sky about the hour of ten. Three times it struck the ear. At first from perhaps a furlong to the south of the camp; then, in ten seconds or so, almost directly overhead; another pause of ten seconds and it came back from the north; then silence. I guessed the wing speed at forty-five to fifty miles per hour. A strong flier was this bird of my Kakahi nights. His flight was always from south to north.

The rarest bird of the river valley was found by a cat in a swamp above the gorge a mile or so upstream from the cottage. Rudi Nuemann, who shared a comfortable farmhouse with six other cats, was a skilled hunter with a scientific bent. To indicate his independence he occasionally left home for weeks at a time and always returned with a good bag. Many times he brought home a wild duckling from the swamp, always carefully, and each time presented it to his mistress Betty. This involved a journey for her through several paddocks back to the swamp. It was no wonder that she released it with a solemn warning to keep out of Master Rudi's way in future.

Another day his mistress saw him trotting confidently across the home paddock bearing in his mouth a tiny rabbit, which she knew she would have the job of skinning for him. Suddenly a hawk swooped down, grabbed bunny junior out of his mouth and was high in the air again before Rudi realised what had happened.

His most famous exploit was the bringing home of a small dark bird. Thinking it was just a blackbird and seeing it was quite dead, his mistress threw it out into the garden. This did not suit Rudi. He found it and returned it to her insisting: "Look, I've got something unusual for you this time." Then Mrs Nuemann looked at it again more carefully and saw that it was not a blackbird. The first thing she noticed was that the nostril was long and she could see right through it; also that the legs were quite different from the blackbird's. Rudi was right. Of course it was something unusual. Word was passed through the township.

The birdlovers were consulted, books of reference were looked up and finally the little bird was identified quite correctly as the Swamp Crake (*porzana plumbea*). When I arrived on the scene it was to find the bird hard frozen in the Nuemann deep freezer. It looked a sad little person, this dark, shy recluse of the dismal swampland. Its total length was only six inches and its weight about three and a half ounces.

I packed the body in a box and posted it to the Wildlife Branch for record. Happening to be in Wellington a little later, I rang the Wildlife Branch and asked permission to speak to the Controller. A voice answered:

"Kelly," it said.

"Kelly," I replied.

A short silence.

"Kelly here."

"Kelly *here*."

A longer silence. I almost heard the brain tick over.

"That you, Greg? You old devil."

"Yes, Henry. Why didn't you answer my letter?"

"Oh, have a heart. It's only three weeks ago."

"I see, Henry, government stroke. Did you give Bob Falla that specimen?"

"I did not. We're mounting it ourselves for our own collection. The only one we've seen. Come and have lunch."

So Rudi's field work concluded as he would have desired — and I got a free lunch.

Henry advised that the local people of Owhango had identified this bird correctly. Its usual title is Spotless Crake. The Maoris call it Puweto. It certainly lives in a weto place.

19. *Disasters are not Impostors*

The bags of trout caught by my rod have not been highlighted in these pages, but it is now the moment to speak of my last fishing holiday at Kakahi before Mount Ruapehu erupted. Both the Wanganui and the Whakapapa rivers were fishing well, with a mixture of browns and rainbows. I camped by the latter stream as usual, and thus could please myself where and when to go out with the rod. The flies were the old team: Cochy, Red-tipped Governor, Purple Jessie, Greenwell's Glory, Twilight Beauty and Hardy's Favourite – with a widespread wing to use in bright sunlight. All except the first and last named were fished wet or dry as conditions required, but mostly dry.

In the twelve days I killed thirty-three first-class fish with an average of three and a half pounds. Most of these were packed in tea-tree cocoons and sent away by rail, quite a simple matter when the guards of the main express trains were kind enough to hang the cocoons in their van so that the cool night air could fan them. A few other fish went to the odd caller or passer-by.

I kept no record of the number of trout which were liberated. These must have equalled those taken. Only two slabs were seen, both rainbow jacks, which were killed and buried.

This kind of angling is something to remember. I had for the most part the rivers to myself.

Threadliners were met in weekends and sometimes spoiled the reaches for the fly, but in spite of them I had all the fun any man could wish for. The weather held well, though the nights were chilly in the tent. Wind is seldom a problem there; in fact it is the calmest place I know, as well as being almost completely free of fog.

A plan had been in my mind for a long time to build a permanent cottage on top of the cliff from which I could look down along the Whakapapa towards its junction with the Wanganui. From there I could see the dawns break over the ranges and, in certain conditions, spirals of steamlike camp-fire smoke rise straight in the still air as far away as Te Rena. One, two, three, sometimes six of these wraiths stood like sentinels against the background of the dark bush range beyond the river, as though they were the camp fires of tough, tattooed warriors who had fought there so savagely, tribe against tribe, in an age that has gone.

That was my plan. Had I been able to foresee the black change that would befall the trout population and ruin the fishing for twenty years, even so, I doubt whether I would have given up my dream-cottage plans. The reason is clear enough. I had been completely captivated by the quality of this calm, peaceful and beautiful district where Nature seemed to rest.

In 1945 black disaster in the form of volcanic ash from the heart of the mountain that had slept so long that it was "extinct", was blown in thousands and thousands of tons across the countryside. The bulk of the mountain's vomit fell on the mountain itself where it must still lie thick awaiting disturbance.

In every yard and deep in every pool of the river, this vile stuff spread a smothering blanket, stifling the life upon which trout, big and small, depend for their food. The breeding redds, where the cleverest of mothers digs in her precious ova which must have oxygen or die, were completely ruined by a cement-like coating.

This is too long a story to pursue in detail. It is enough to say that the glorious fishing we had had for so long fell away and away and away. An ichthyologist of fame came to Kakahi and examined the disaster area. Turning to a friend of mine he said: "It will take twenty years to recover from this eruption." Twenty years! Was it credible?

On several holiday trips to my camping site in the years following the eruption, I found it was almost useless looking for a rise in the Whakapapa. The only fishing for me was along the upper reaches of the Wanganui above the junction. From there to the pool at Te Rena, where I caught my first Kakahi fish, there were good trout of both species to be taken at almost any part of the day with the dry fly. Friends, not all dry-fly men, also had similar experiences. Below the junction the fishing of the Wanganui was also spoiled for many miles by the ash carried down from the Whakapapa. Local anglers found it was more profitable to go either to the Taupo district or north to the Ongarue River which flows south to join the Wanganui at Taumarunui.

The glory had departed from the Whakapapa's angling; the improvement was slow in coming. Flood water always brought down fresh deposits of the volcanic ash from the mountain's sides and slopes. The mountain was being sluiced of its dirt by every hard rainfall and every gutter-cleaning spate in the river itself. By early 1948 it was possible to raise an odd fish in the Apron and Skipper's pools, as well as along the more level stretches between the gorge and Whakapapa island. This provided most exciting fishing as one was never sure at any time whether fish were present or not.

By 1952 my wife and I had decided to build a permanent home where my old fishing house had been. The ensuing eight years saw a gradual improvement, year by year, in the fishing. But, at the end of that time, it was still far below its pre-eruption splendour. At times we had floods of the usual kind. I called them the ash-wash floods. All to the good.

From our bedroom window we could listen to the babbling of the river; it was pleasant, soothing, lulling. When the song of the waters altered and almost fell away to silence, we knew spates from the mountain had risen, covering the conversational stones and boulders. We knew when daylight came again we would see the river swollen, turbid, unfishable and, as our water-pump was there, also unpumpable.

As a rule this river clears rapidly and its rages are of short duration. In February 1958, we saw something different. This was the year of a disaster which was to tear the life out of the river and undo all its upward struggle to recover from the eruption damage. Other rivers than ours were badly mauled by this outsized flood. The Tongariro pools of history were devastated; property damage over the whole of the King Country was heartbreaking.

Early on the morning of February 24 the Taumarunui Borough Council telephoned:

"Mr Kelly, how is the river below your house? The Château manager, Mr Dennis, tells us they have had eight inches of rain during the night."

"Well, the river is pretty wild," I told them. "Logs and trees as well as rafts of pumice bank are floating past. Water is coming over the decking of Rex Smith's bridge, and the water is still rising."

"Thank you. Will you advise us if it gets much worse please?"

"Gladly, so long as the telephone lasts."

"We might have to evacuate people from their homes in Matapuna."

It did get worse. I had the sad task of passing the warning. My wife and I saw at nine forty-five the fine new bridge over the river struck with a mighty totara tree. The great thing came down like a battering-ram, roots foremost, its giant five-foot diameter log forty feet long, backed by its massive tops and many tons of pumice and other debris behind, making it an irresistible force. It struck the side of the bridge, already loaded with logs, stumps and broken trees, with a dull shuddering thud. The bridge sagged *upstream* like a rolling ship and the raging waters poured over it. When daylight came again the whole structure was gone. Only the top of one pylon showed.

The slow up-build of our trout fishing went with the bridge. The singing waters below the house were gone. My shrine, the Apron, was gone. A tree leaned wearily over the grave.

A week later when I saw the towns of Te Kuiti and Otorahanga many miles north with fences festooned with bedding, furniture piled high in the main street, people waiting for their homes to dry out, dead sheep and cattle in the gullies, I knew that fishermen had little to moan about.

This is fine medicine, and Doctor Nature knows well how to use it. Small trout grow into big trout, time and food allowing. Rivers have a way, too, of forming new pools and making good places for their splendid tenants. Our fish losses earned us sympathy from the acclimatisation societies which made generous liberations.

Records of the Whakapapa are meagre, but there is confirmation of what I found in the visitors' book at "Te Whare Ra", a historic camp established in 1920 by the late William Henry Wilson, Esq., of Wanganui, next to the twenty acres where I built my own.

Douglas Earle, an experienced angler, also from Wanganui, has written many interesting comments in its pages:

> 1958 April. After THE FLOOD most of the time was spent exploring and finding the river, and how to get to it. Amazing to relate, we still got fish out of the Wanganui. Largest 4 pounds.
>
> 1959 December. Fishing full of interest. Party landed nine out of fifteen hooked, weighing $1\frac{3}{4}$ to 4 lbs. All in perfect condition.
>
> 1960 April. No takeable fish in the Whakapapa, but full of little fellows. Wanganui still had a number of heavy fish. Mrs Richardson caught a beautiful $5\frac{1}{4}$ lb hen rainbow on a No 8 Twilight Beauty.

1960 October. Fighting for position with hordes of bait-casters.

December. River discoloured. One takeable fish.

1962 April. 12 fish, largest 3½ lbs all taken on the fly. Sept–Oct 'trip'. 1 day's fishing, then rained. 3 nice fish. More rods on the river than ever seen before, during the day they were all using ironmongery.

1962 Dec. 26 to Jan. 3. No fishing for first three days till river fell. Fish a bit larger than usual. 3 were over 3 lbs. Only one fish was taken in evening.

1963 Easter. A week's fishing. Bag, a few hard-luck stories. Locals say it has been no good since Jan. Few rods.

Dec. Peter Wilson of Wanganui caught the best fish seen since the War, a 6 lb brown, condition factor 63·7. From the 24th to the 31st the fishing was patchy. Then came the rain.

A few other details from the visitors' book show that E. G. Webber and Peter McIntyre formed an echelon with their families in 1960. The echelon captured twenty-six fish in nine days, six of which were over three pounds, caught mostly on tiny nymphs or small Red-tipped Governors.

Five years later the E. G. Webbers and the Neil Blundells recorded that the two best fish taken by them were a six-pound brown and a five-and-a-half pounder.

Last night (November 1, 1966) I fished a pool in the Wanganui at Kakahi with Jim Lawn and Bill Edgar. Using the dry pukeko I missed two fish in the broken water through being over eager. When too dark to see the dry, I changed to the Twilight nymph, losing two fish before hooking and landing a good three-pound brown and another of one and three-quarter pounds. My fish surprised me by their vigour. The former tore off twenty or more yards of line and jumped high at the end of the first run. Though I was sure the gentle take of the nymph was that of a brown, the way this fish fought almost persuaded me that I had hooked a rainbow.

When my companions rejoined me they had ten fish, five each. So in all we had taken twelve trout in less than two hours. Lawn used a Purple Jessie, but I did not ask his friend and pupil what he had used.

Our flashlight made a charming and interesting picture of the fish as they were lying on a shelf of rich green grass beside the pool. There was only one under a pound, all the others were from one and three-quarters to three pounds. All except one, a two-pound rainbow, were brownies.

The following day I drove down into the deep gorge of the Whakapapa by way of a new road cut through standing native forest that is as it was before the days of Captain Cook. The ancient silent stillness of old New Zealand grips the heart in this small remnant of what was a mighty and some-times terrifying wilderness of dense greenery where only birds could find their way. Fine specimens of matai, rimu, totara, tawa and white pine stand clean and straight with under-growth of wineberry, fivefinger, and fuchsia shading their feet. Vines climb and cling to the limbs and upper canopy. Clematis were hanging out hymeneal veils for the brides that were not there.

At the bottom, where the bridge reaches across, an entrancing picture lies in wait almost to shock the senses with its pure riverine beauty. From the sideless bridge one can see a cascading volume of snow-born water hurrying through the gorge in two separate streams. The main one plunges over a wide barrier of solid rock that twists it to the left and again to the right to steady before it passes under the bridge. The falls themselves, though small, as indeed the beautiful stream itself is small, turn the water into a chromo of white, blue, light green and dark. Part of the floor of rock is tawny and wrinkled, contrasting strongly with the black and green rock of the rest.

Downstream the river runs a straight passage through the

high forested walls at a fast pace, but without white water. Pools seem to pause here and there; small pumice beaches lodge at intervals. The pools look tempting and good. This is the living Whakapapa. Truda sent me down to the falls so that a photo could be taken. I took my little Walker rod and tied on a snobby Greenwell's Glory and cast under the lip of the nearest fall. A large rainbow bolted from under the rock on which I was standing and disappeared in the blue water. At once two little ones came up out of the deep and swam into a calm pool on my left. Truda waved that the camera had clicked and I came away reluctantly.

As we took our farewell of the Whakapapa I wondered how long this truly glorious stream has to live before the third and final disaster falls? How long does it take for a river to be diverted through tunnels to where God never intended?

20. "Fantastic Fishing"

In the Taupo district is the only privately owned water in the Dominion. The owners charge a pretty stiff fee for the privilege of fishing there, and this might be the reason for the water being more lightly fished than "open" waters.

My introduction to Lake Rotoaira was due to the kindness of my friend Les Mark of Taumarunui. He had often spoken to me about the quality of the trout and their abundance when inviting me to go with him to sample what the lake had to offer.

It was in December 1960 that we left Taumarunui after breakfast to travel the sixty-odd miles to the lake. I was glad Les chose the way over the Waituhi Saddle across the Hauhangaroa Range through changing scenery. At first we drove through the more developed farming land where prosperous farms have been carved out of the wilderness left from sawmilling days. Stumps, logs, second growth and weeds had to be overcome and green pastures established in their stead. Many of these farms make fine pictures when viewed from the road which winds up the Punga-Punga incline towards the more open grasslands where lesser bush growth had been removed. Farther on the road leads through the reserved and ancient rain forest where a wise administration retains control over a quarter-mile green band through which the highway runs. Splendid specimens of rimu, totara, matai and white pine stand tall and clean to reflect the past glory of a great paradise of primeval forest.

At one spot the driver stopped and we got out of the car to look down and over rumpled acres of untouched bush to the far ranges and the tips of Ruapehu and Ngauruhoe, still snow clad on this December day.

Les turned off the highway at Ruamata and drove along a sawmill company's private road through their cut-over bush. He said that this saved five miles of travel, though I felt he was as pleased as I was that it offered more than a short cut. Surely in a place like this the rich fecundity of the New Zealand countryside has a breathing example. All the big trees with a millable log had been cut down, but lesser trees had been left. Bastard birch, tawhera, rewarewa, lacebark and tawa held their heads up to support vines and shelter new growth which sprang from nowhere to cover the scars left by the bushmen. Soon the dead tops of the milled trees and the smaller ones inevitably crushed by falling tree and by tractor would rot down into fertile soil to nourish the wild growth of wineberry, ferns of all kinds and every other green thing that found a footing there.

In these miles square of cut-out bush country there are red deer, wild pigs, hares, and – say it in a whisper – rabbits. The hares are very fond of this place and we saw nine crossing the track in the five miles we drove through.

Soon we reached the lake. The theory was that the ranger who lived there would provide me with the necesssary permit to fish. Les had a full season permit as well as a Taupo licence, both types being necessary. The ranger was not there and had not arranged a stand-in. So there was to be no fishing for me. All I could do was to sit in the boat and watch my friend catch the fish. We left the landing in Les's own boat with the one rod. At first he thought we should hang about the landing in the hope that the ranger would return. We went first to the water tower, which registers the levels of the lake, from where we could see the landing. Here a small fish or two indicated that this was not a satisfactory place, so I persuaded Les to go to his "better 'oles" up the lake.

The lake itself is quite unspoiled. As far as could be seen

from the water, there is not much, if any, cultivation along the banks. All along the southern bank, which is high, rock-walled, and richly overgrown, my friend cruised in the little boat with its small outboard motor. He knew every inch in this run of something over two miles. So we put-putted slowly from "good spots" to "ought-to-be-good" ones to stop here, to stop there. Each stop meant lowering the anchor as quietly as possible. When that spot was exploited a move was made to another.

In most of these spots the angler had action. Two beauties were in the boat by the time we reached the "sure-thing" water. Here I saw three splendid trout hooked within five minutes of one another. Two of these were boated, the other managed to get rid of the hook. All were in the four-pound class and all gave great displays.

It was lunch time and we pulled the boat up an inlet and soon had the thermette boiler going. Les grilled the first trout caught over a tiny fire of tea-tree embers, merely using a square bit of wire netting as a griller. He simply slit the fish down the back from head to tail and drew the halves apart, exposing gills, liver, heart and all the rest which were lifted out. This left the fish clean with belly skin intact. Setting the body, skin downwards, on the wire netting, he placed the fish on the glowing embers and that was all. The fish, though slightly underdone, was delicious. All the natural juices were there because the fish had not been turned. I now saw the cook's wisdom in not splitting the fish down the belly; the juices would have been lost. It was also obvious why he had avoided turning the grill.

Back to the boat and the one-sided fishing. Les fished all along towards the top of the lake where a stream, the Wai-rehu, enters. The fish had gone off for a time, and it was an hour or more before anything happened. It was then we had the pleasure of watching the bird-life around us, for the lake and its margins are a wild-life refuge where even the cor-morants and the hawks are safe. We saw two large rafts of the

The author fishing the
Apron Pool in the
Whakapapa River

The author with the
limit at Lake Rotoaira

Whakapapa Gorge

little black teal who had no fear of us. Grey ducks were also numerous, but kept their distance. We saw two black-backed gulls and a few wisps of pied stilt.

Then we found that the trout were on the job again and so Les concentrated on his casting. Finally he caught his eighth trout to make his legal limit for the day and we were soon on our way back to the landing.

Almost at once we were struck in the face by one of those sudden squalls that make boating risky on freshwater lakes like Rotoaira. White-capped waves appeared like magic and tossed the small craft about like a cork. It was unpleasant to feel the boat lifted high and then smack down again with an explosive shudder as the stern kicked up and the propeller missed. Water slopped over the bows in spite of my efforts to fend off the waves with my waterproof fishing cape.

This was a bad moment for something to go wrong; the motor cut out. I saw Les groping in the bilge water at his feet for something while I battled with one oar to keep bows on into the wind. At the next moment we were in peril of being bashed on to the house-sized rocks. However, Les found what he was groping for, a bit of wire that had fallen off the ignition plug. Instantly the brave little Seagull started and we were on our way once again. Ten minutes and she coughed out again.

"Aw, the tank's empty, Greg," Les remarked calmly. "Chuck us that tin from under the bow counter, will you?"

I did. But again we were back to the rocks and I was busy with the oar to fend away from them. Les with the tank stopper gripped in his teeth was using both hands to try to fill the buck-jumping tank, spilling a lot in the tide, but getting some where it was wanted.

Faithfully the engine responded to the starting cord and we were free of the rocks only to be halted again. This time the motor would not respond to many pulls till I yelled: "Open the air vent, Les."

"Aw, yes o'course, Greg," came the calm reply.

H

It was marvellous to feel the lift of the small engine as she jumped again into her job. Soon we battled round a headland into the quieter water of a bay. The next minute, it seemed, the squall was over, and as suddenly as it lost its temper the lake was smooth again. We reached the landing at ten minutes to six. The ranger had not returned.

Two days later we were back at the primitive lake. This time, the ranger was there and I was able to buy authority to fish. The day was fair with just enough movement in the air to break up the glassy glare which is fatal to this kind of fishing. Les drove the boat well up the lake near where the fish had been active last time. When we anchored and paid out a bit of rope, the boat swung round in the slight breeze and rode steadily. Acting on my mate's advice I mounted a Turkey and Red size four, and to my astonishment I hooked a fish on my first cast, a hen of about two pounds. "That's the stuff!" Les shouted gleefully. "I told you I'd show you some fantastic fishing."

From then on for quite a short period we got patches of strikes. Some half-dozen of these were released as being under the fourteen-inch limit, and some others were missed or lost.

There was no need to grieve here for a fish lost, for the fresh offers were numerous.

"Seems like your silly trout are just waiting down there with their mouths open, Les."

It did seem like this, as several times we were both playing fish at the same time. On these occasions Les shouted with the abandon of a schoolboy cheering his team for a concerted try. "Come on, mate," he would chant, as he whipped one in over the boat, and then gave the net a deft flip to throw the "mate" out. Grabbing it by the tail, he used a rowlock as a priest. Whack, whack, whack. "This hurts me more than it hurts you, mate. How many is that?" to me.

"You have three to go, Les. I have three and five to go. We have eight beautiful fish. Can we call it a day?"

"Not on your lifebuoy. I promised you the limit, you

know." So we plugged our way to the top of the lake, where there was a rough sort of landing, for lunch.

Again my friend prepared a beautiful trout for grilling while I lit a small fire to boil the thermette and make grilling embers. While we were doing this a "bomb" truck arrived down a roadway through the bush. Out stepped three young Maoris. Though they could hardly have been aware of it, they were the originals of the long-haired and bearded young men so fashionable now. They were genial fellows with the natural grace and good manners of their race. They eyed the fire and the big trout grilling there in silence.

"What are you fellows after?"

"Oh, nothing. We just look round, eh."

"Do you intend fishing?"

"No, we doan go fishing. I doan like fishing myself. Take too many patience."

His reasoning was quite sound, I thought, though I still wondered. One of the lads went down to the edge of the water and dangled his legs over the bank. The other two just sat and yarned to each other. Les and I soon got busy with our food as we had had an early breakfast. There was, of course, more fish than we could manage. Les said, "Come and have a bit of fish, if you would like it." Both agreed and came forward. Immediately the leg-dangler came up and joined his mates.

"My word, water too cold for a paddle, eh."

They didn't like fishing, perhaps, but grilled trout was a different matter. As we came away, and they got their billy out of the truck, they promised me they would douse our fire before they left. I'm quite sure that they would. After all, this was their country and their forest.

By the time we reached one of the other favoured spots a change had come over the weather, and a cold south-westerly air-stream blew in on the lake. It was not strong, but it was chilly. At odd times light misty showers also came over. Added to this discomfort, the fishing became harder. Les had his limit at five minutes past four, but I was still two short, and was not caring much. I had injured my right leg and now, with the cold wind and wet feet, it was playing up a bit.

"Stick to it, kid," Les urged. "You must get that limit."

"Right. I'll give it another hour."

This would bring the time to about five-fifteen. I was longing to get another look at the Ruamata track through the bush, and time was running out. I landed my seventh fish at four-thirty. One to go! I missed two others before finally hooking a solid fish that did everything except get rid of the hook. Les lifted the lovely fighter into the boat and extended his powerful right hand to congratulate me on my first limit. My first ever.

We reached the Ruamata road while yet the summer evening light was holding. My fine old Brno rifle accounted for a hare in the first half mile. I counted twelve more on our way through the bush.

Then Les spotted a red deer hind slipping quietly down a logging track, but she was able to elude him without trouble. As we were moving about searching we had the thrill of seeing an albino tui fly across the roadway. Its rump and tail-feathers were snow white. This was the first albino tui either of us had seen. It flew into a thick mass of greenery and we were unable to locate it again. Ten minutes later when we were near the main highway a hind walked sedately down the road, entering the bush to our left. In a matter of seconds Les was out of the car and on its track. Soon a shot rang out to shatter the silence for a moment. There was nothing I could do but sit and wait. Within minutes the angler-hunter was back to the car with the rear half of a fat maiden hind on his shoulder.

When we reached the top of the Hauhangaroa Range at the Waituhi trig, we found that snow had been falling, so it was no wonder that we had felt chilly on the lake.

So ended the second day.

Rump
& Tail feathers
Snow White

Fly Dressing UGLY Duckling

21. The Ugly Duckling

One of the flies in my hat is surely the ugly duckling of the party. Though it resembles no fly, nymph or caddis in my judgement, it has proved its worth as a killer when more orthodox patterns failed to interest the fish.

It was developed by John Sierpinski of Rainbow Point, Taupo. It is the simplest thing one ever saw. As I look at the sample in my hat this is how it appears to be dressed: to a size five eyed Limerick hook with turned down eye is bound alternate bands of black and red ordinary darning wool, starting at the eye. First black, of which three strands stand upright a quarter of an inch; then red, black again and so on. As the wool is turned on, wisps of black fuzzy fur from the tail of a possum are taken in sparingly, a small whisk of this being left protruding at the tail. That's all. There are no wings and no hackle, as we regard hackle.

Like any other fly, this one has to be fished in its own way and, as it is a sinking type, experience in its retrieving motion and timing is of importance. John has caught scores, if not hundreds, of fish on it in a season.

One evening in November 1963, I was present when John was among those fishing at Kuratau Spit on the South Western shores of Lake Taupo. We were all getting some sport; but by eight o'clock John's score of four was the highest. As fishing in the dark is not one of my joys, I returned to the cottage with my two fish.

So I was not there when John had an accident. This is his account of it related to me after his recovery:

"I had four fish, but kept on as they were still biting. I

was trying to get out as far as I could, so made an extra effort. I think the wind caught my line because I felt a blow in my right eye. My own fly had done it. The pain made me call out and drop my rod. I thought my eye was torn out.

"An angler fishing near came running up. 'I'm a doctor. Can I help you?'

"That was lucky. He said: 'Your eye is still there; but the hook has gone. The hook has missed the pupil, but has cut the lid and the eyeball as it flew forward, just slashing it.'

"The doctors and nurses made a good job of me, and now this small scar is all you can see. My eye is as good as ever."

"Now, I tell you something," he continued. "You won't believe it. When one of the fishermen picked up my rod to wind the line in, there was a fish on my fly!"

It surely must be uncommon for an angler to hook himself and a fish with the same fly on the same cast.

There could be an explanation of the fish being on the hook. Plainly this fly or lure sinks to the bottom in slack water, given time. When the injury was being attended to, the rod was on the sand, and the slack line in the water. When being wound in, probably smartly, the lure would be jerked off the bottom and then grabbed by a fish. Any other conclusion seems doubtful because the hooked fish would have ripped off the line, and perhaps have dragged the loose rod into the lake.

This idea intrigued me, and I asked John if he'd allow me to go fishing with him so that I could observe his method of using this successful fly of his.

To this he readily agreed, and now that he has kindly done so, I'll relate what happened.

The day was beautifully fine and mild for mid-April when John telephoned:

"Have you been to prison?" was his startling question.

"Well, only a little, John," I replied, "and then on visits."

"Have you feeshed the Waiotaka there?"

The penny dropped.

"Oh, I see what you mean," I said. "No. I once visited the old camp to see some friends who were fishing there."

"Well, could you get a permit to go today?"

"I don't know, John. Perhaps. We could apply."

We drove the thirty odd miles to the Hauto prison farm. When I stated our case and established identity, permission was granted.

The permits granted are printed cards setting out the reasonable conditions.

"Mr Rogers suggests you go to the Cliff Pool. It is well signposted," Guardsman Gill told me.

We found the stream to be rather low and very, very clear. Good sized trout could be seen lying along the bottom and not feeding, John rigged up my rod, tying on a short cast to which one of his green ducklings was tied on a size four hook. I was not in a hurry to start, as his method of fishing his patent fly was my chief interest at that moment.

He stood at the top of the reach and cast straight downstream, then just kept still without moving the line. After about a minute his left hand began a slow recovery of line in irregular movements, with an occasional pause of, perhaps, ten seconds.

Almost at once he hooked and lost a fish. This astonished me as it was my view that the fish were not "on the feed".

For the next three hours we saw fish in every pool, all lying on the bottom, black against the light sand and gravel. Not one took any notice of our best efforts except to bolt if we ventured too close.

I fished John's patterns faithfully as a pupil could, admitting to myself what a poor hand I was at this wet-fly type of fishing.

In one pool only did I try to fish the ugly one as a nymph, and succeeded in persuading a trout of about two pounds to follow it down the current; but he made no attempt to take it. Of course he saw me and fled.

I'm not persistent in this discouraging business and sat down in a shady place to relax.

My friend had gone downstream and I had had a fair rest by the time he rejoined me.

"Any good, Greg?"

"No, John, not a damn thing."

"They won't make up their mind to take it," was his odd remark. "Come, we have some tea."

In comparing notes, we estimated we had seen fifty or sixty fish, all apparently of takeable size and of untakeable appetite.

After tea, John returned to his first reach and moved down that very attractive water again with unvarying methods.

I fished from the same point upstream. All the way I used the upstream cast, with John's Ugly Duckling fished as a nymph.

Then I arrived at a notice board reading:

"FLOOD-GATE — CLIFF" with an arrow — not a broad one — pointing upstream.

Then I came upon what was obviously the cliff pool, which is the largest we saw that day. It is long, wide and very deep against the far bank, that is, the right-hand bank. This water seemed to be the sort John liked, so it was left for him and I went further up to another nice piece of river.

Here, with the use of Polaroid glasses, I saw several large fish lying, just like the others seen earlier, like logs at the bottom and felt that it was useless trying for them at that stage. I sat down on a grassy bank and waited.

It was now about a quarter to six and if fish were going to rise, it would have to be soon.

The head of this pool was wide and the surface of the water was broken by a ridge of stones which turned the current slightly away from my side of the river. It made a perfect dry-fly spot if the trout would rise.

It was completely absorbing to sit in this quiet place.

No sign of man; no sign of industry. The mild air was

clean and fresh. Several fantails flitted along the blackberry and sedges; bellbirds kept their chorus in their spasmodic way.

Thoughts of where I was could not be excluded. This place was a prison. Within its boundaries, and perhaps not far away, were men who for some strange reason of their own failed to live within the law of this beautiful land of peace and plenty.

Then my eye caught a movement in the water. A large brown trout had moved into position ten yards or so below the rainbows. He was hungry, it seemed, and weaved from side to side.

I thought of trying to coax him to the surface, so removed John's Ugly Duckling and tied on a dry Bloody Butcher which Red Spinner had tied for me as a gift last year, but which had never interested any fish I offered it to in the Tuki Tuki, Whakapapa or the Rai.

Getting ready to cast to the big brownie, I realised he was a slab!

"Great Scott!" I said. "I might have ruined the pool with you."

This was lucky, as almost at once a fish rose on the edge of the white water. I oiled the Bloody Butcher which, by the way, is tied with a fiery red tail and a long silver body with a sparse brush of stiff shiny black hackles like a Queen Bess ruff near the eye, and sent it on its mission.

The cast and line appeared to come down to the right and snaked nicely. In a second or two there was a swirl on the surface and my rod curved thrillingly as I tightened on the fish.

I drew her quietly enough, but perhaps too firmly, down stream below the "lie" before she went mad. So after she made three leaps in the air I felt she was mine, but the line suddenly went slack.

Oh well, everyone knows about the one that got away.

Nothing to do now but to sit down again for ten minutes.

The fly was wiped dry and re-oiled; even the line got a rub down with a float-line pad.

A single spinner fell almost at my feet. That was the only one I saw.

John was fishing the cliff pool by this time and I felt sure that he would take a fish there — at least I hoped he would.

Then to my joy I saw another fish rise in the broken water and stood up to have a go at him. My first cast was short of the spot and too far to the right; but the next went according to plan and was accepted boldly.

This time the fish was handled with more caution and came down the water with a wild rush. She leapt in the air and fought fiercely. The scream of the reel must have brought John to the scene.

That fish jumped clear of the water five times, and the last was a good four-footer. Once again the reel screamed and as I ran to recover the line, a blackberry vine tripped me and I was prone on a thick mat of grass. I thought my fish was gone, but the hook held. A few minutes later John flipped her out on the grass with his boot.

He removed the dry fly from her throat and remarked that she was securely hooked.

"A beautiful fish!" He killed and bled it. When weighed at home she scaled three and a half pounds.

This fish was packed full of roe, and she was clearly at the point of spawning. Her gut was empty except for some milky slime in which there were two pieces of rock, each the size of a pea. The white stuff could have been, and probably was, milt; the bits of rock might have been gobbled up as she swallowed the milt. So we got no information on the fly upon which the fish were feeding on that occasion.

Our next bit of fishing was a week later at the mouth of the Hatepe River fourteen miles south of Taupo town. We got there about three-thirty and found the lake quiet with a slightly ruffled surface. As at many river mouths, the running water makes straight for the lake; but the solid resistance of the big water which is often carrying pressure of a breeze turns the stream along the shore for a short distance. This current is the hot spot for fish looking for land food being brought down.

Using the Ugly Ducklings again, we fished this current. The sun was bright and warm. John complained about sand-fly bites.

"Don't they bite you, Greg?"

"Perhaps an odd one does, John. They do not worry me."

Why this is the case I do not know. I had been thinking of other bites and had not noticed these either. Was I out of luck?

"I've got one! A feesh! A feesh!"

Sure enough John had a bent rod and his capture finally came ashore—a rainbow jack of three and three quarter pounds. He was in fine condition and full of milt. In his gut was a single carp-shaped fish an inch long and partly digested; but nothing else.

That was the only fish taken up to six p.m. when I left to come home. By four-fifteen we had four other rods to right and left. The one nearest to me, wielded by a powerful arm, went whoof, whoof past my left ear. No one touched a fish in that time, though it was plain that these people were capable anglers.

John came with me to the car and saw me off, insisting I take the fish.

"I'll get more before eleven o'clock!" he said cheerfully.

By that time he would have been standing in the water in his waders almost continuously for over seven hours!

Is this the patience fishermen are supposed to need or is it just physical endurance of a high order?

One thing consoles me. I have seen John catch a fish on his extraordinary fly. My turn will surely come.

22. *All They Got was the Ride*

When my wife and I decided to go to the South Island in the autumn of last year it was second nature to pack our lightest rods and tackle.

As our purpose on this journey was to visit Lake Ellesmere to observe the bird-life there, the "snobby bunch" took second place as we drove south. The fascination of seeing a herd of seals, enormous flights of sea birds, and stunning clouds of Canada geese edged out my secret, almost sacred addiction to fly fishing.

Even though we crossed many fine trout streams it was not possible to wet a cast on the way south. On the return trip we were to stay with the Eric Barkers at Blenheim. This was an area full of promise and Eric knows the waters of the Rai, Pelorus, Wairau and Lake Rotoiti well. "When you get to Blenheim," I said to my snobby bunch, "you can have some trout to get your hooks into if you behave properly."

Our first trip was to the Rai. We paused at the Trout Hotel at Canvastown, so I could get a day's licence. We should have been away weaving our rods over the river in a matter of minutes; but no one, unless he goes for grog alone, can visit the Trout Hotel without being caught up in the interest of this historic spot.

Canvastown. The very name suggests its origin – gold. Redolent of romance and drama, fulfilled dreams and shattered hopes. Hundreds of thousands of pounds worth of the stuff feverishly sought for and fought for, even to murder. The old pattern of the goldfield all over the world.

Then the discovery of real wealth – the land. So with

Canvastown. A solid, steady community with a fixed population celebrated its centenary in 1964 by building a
memorial near the Trout Hotel to the founders of the gold
industry. This memorial includes a collection of the tools
and implements. Among the items, which are set in concrete,
is a big pelton wheel driven by the water power of the stream.
Other tools noticed were an axe head, a set of shoes of
draught-horse size, curiously upside down, a single furrow
plough, a pair of hames of buggy type and a single hame
for draught work.

After the proprietor had issued our licences, Eric said,
"Come into the main bar and I'll show you the biggest
collection of mugs in New Zealand."

I glanced around nervously hoping no one had overheard
what he had said; but there was no trouble. He pushed the
door open and we were struck with a *de profundis* murmur-
ation which came from under a pall of smoke. It was the
buzzing of innumerable beers.

My companion pointed to the ceiling and I saw what he
had meant by mugs. There were scores and scores of them
hanging from hooks on the ceiling; from front to back and
from side to side. They were beautiful in their many kinds
and colours. Surely the collection of a lifetime. Of course
they will never be seen on any hotel bar again, I thought
ruefully.

As we came out of the front door I had a good look at the
enormous red trout let into the rubber door-mat. Was it to
be the only trout I was to see that day?

After a drive of about fifteen miles we came to the Rai.
The road gives ready access to some good trout reaches.
Eric stopped at one point about a hundred yards from the
stream. "This is it," he said. "There are good fish on this
stretch."

It was four o'clock when we got there. Afternoon tea
baskets were unpacked close to a length of beautiful water.
Time was running out as Eric and I finally moved to the

water, and haste is fatal when fishing. So it was my clumsy approach to a lovely pool which cost me the chance at the only fish seen. He saw me first, and took off upstream at speed, to be seen no more. From the position he was in it is almost certain that he was feeding. I judged his weight at three pounds.

Two pools above were flattish and shallow. These I fished with extreme care with a size fourteen Cochy but there was no response. I was tying on a Twilight when I heard a voice calling: "Time to go now, dear." Eric also heard the call, and we met on the bank where we had parted. He had nothing to report as we turned reluctantly away from the pleasant Rai River.

Time. Time. Time. There's never enough time!

Our second foray was up the Wairau Valley to Lake Rotoiti, a distance of some sixty-odd miles. The road parallels the river most of the way, and I do not know a trout stream anywhere with such ready access for so great a distance. At one point Eric stopped the car.

"There's a big fish in that pool. Several have seen him; but no one can catch him. Better not pause to try your luck now if we want to reach the lake while the weather is good."

When we arrived at the lake there was much to see: the lake itself, set like a jewel in a ring of mountains dominated by Mount Robert, beckoning tracks through the birch forest. Being an old deerstalker it was impossible for me to pass by the spendid Red Deer Lodge which the Nelson members of the Deerstalkers' Association have built close to the lake. This is no hunters' shelter with a tin chimney and a bench outside. It is built like the wing of a modern hotel with an all-electric kitchen and a magnificent lounge which holds some of the great and historic heads of a vanished day. The floor space covers over 2,000 square feet, and quarters are provided for members' families.

We were very interested in the shelters for public use built by the National Park Board. These are a great boon to hunters, trampers, fishermen and picnickers. It was one of the electric stoves in the well-equipped units of one of these shelters that further delayed a chance to fish. It was only after the loss of several shillings, followed by a thump, that the thermometer very slowly started to show a rise in oven temperature. No bacon-and-egg pie has ever heated so slowly. We suspected the stoves had been cruelly treated by the use of washers instead of shillings.

However, there was still an hour or two left to fish the mighty Buller River at its source. At this spot, on this day, it was truly a wonderful piece of dry-fly water.

Again a day's licence was called for as we were now in the Nelson area, but Ranger Lyon was absent. We were told: "No day licence, only weekly at fifteen shillings each."

I recalled Sandy Monahan's remark about the five-fish daily limit: "We don't want Wellington fellows to come here to skin out our rivers."

I wondered how good the Wellington anglers were supposed to be, by the Nelson Acclimatisation councillors. Or whether, like the mighty admiral himself, they were one-eyed. No licence: no fishing!

"Come on," Eric said, "we have day licences for Marlborough. Let's go back to the Wairau."

We stopped again by a piece of swamp, at Betty's request. "I want some tadpoles, Eric. This is where I got the last lot for our fish pond."

Donning gummies the women stalked their tadpoles, while Eric and I got our fish poles rigged. We moved to the pool where the legendary big one was.

"You have a go at him, Greg. He lies deep under the near bank."

It sounded like a challenge.

As rainbows are rare in South Island rivers which have a sea outlet, it was probable that this fish was a brownie. As the browns do not rise well in the daytime as a rule, I tied on one of John's Ugly Ducklings on a number six hook and used a length of seven-and-a-half-pound breaking strain nylon, and cast downstream. There is a trick in this kind of deep-fly casting which has won me quite a few strikes of both brown and rainbow. When the line has almost straightened, a yard or two of loose line is allowed to slip between finger and thumb of the left hand, a little, say a foot, at a time, until the line is straight below. Long-line casting is not necessary.

In this case it worked and I was rewarded with a heavy strike. In fact it was a jolt. I had no doubt it was Eric's big 'un. Whether the jolt did it or not, I could not blame myself but the next moment the line went slack.

I tried all the other tricks one usually uses, such as changing flies, resting the pool, leaving the fly to rest on the bottom before retrieving, but no other touch was felt. Eric rejoined me from the upper pools. He had taken and released a small one. I told him my tale; I hope he believed it.

We went back for Betty and my wife and their three tadpoles. They had more to show for their efforts than we had. Then we drove back to Blenheim to a mighty dinner, Liebfraumilch, and Beethoven's No. 5 to console us.

Archie Caldwell fishing Blackberry Bar on the Whakapapa River

Young fisherman at Whakaipo Bay, Lake Taupo

23. Whakamaru Fighters

Just before we left Taumarunui to live in Taupo in 1963 a friend gave me a large chicken-like fly known as Parson's Glory.

"This," he said, "Mr Jim Birnie of the Spa Hotel considers is the best fly to use on the Waikato."

The other flies in my hat must have received somewhat of a shock at its arrival on their stomping ground. Its inventor was unknown to me; but I hope he receives his full measure of glory for his creation, as this monstrous fly brought me my first rainbow from Lake Whakamaru, a large man-made lake on the Waikato River.

The lake is twenty miles from Tokoroa, that sudden town of 14,000 which the conversion of pine trees into some 120 kinds of paper at Kinleith has brought into existence.

Christmas of 1965 saw us comfortably settled in a motel at Tokoroa. One of the delightful roads traversed pine forests, through which sunlight filtered to dapple ferny glades of reconstituted growth. It led to Lake Whakamaru and the Waikato River below Atiamuri. Promising angling water made my palm itch to use a trout rod.

Learning of my weakness, the captain of the Tokoroa Fresh Water Angling Club, Rob Walker, arranged a trip.

"I'll call for you at five a.m. tomorrow. I think you will like the early morning rise."

I'm not sure whether this meant me or the Whakamaru trout. Anyway, I was up through the wee sma' oors to look at the weather. By this time it was made up of howling blasts and heavy showers. The prospects were anything but

I

propitious for angling, and boat fishing was the last thing to consider.

Faithful to arrangements, Rob Walker knocked on the door of our flat at five minutes to five, just as I was sipping my second cup of tea.

Instead of saying, as I had expected he would, that it was too rough for our twenty-mile journey, the young man was smiling happily at our prospects!

"It will be all right down there," he said. "You'll see."

Conditions improved and we found the water reasonably fishable. My host rowed the boat out a hundred yards from the bank and cast the anchor, a brick, overboard. Rob noticed my questioning look.

"Can't beat a brick. It holds better in the weeds."

"Weeds!"

Big patches of weeds below the surface made knowledge of the water imperative. Rob knew the location of these spots and as far as I could gather had anchored the boat where the weeds were not too close to the surface to be dangerous to casting. He knew fish get food from or around the banks of weeds.

Before I mounted the recommended fly — it is a lure rather than a fly — it was necessary to remove the tapered dry-fly cast with its 3x point and beg a length of heavier gut from my host. To this I tied the Glory and started work. All these preparations were made on my host's advice.

The boat swung on its brick anchor from right to left and jobbled up and down in the wind-scuffed water. I sat in the bow and cast back towards the bank.

An odd fish was still seen to be rising. My watch indicated six-twenty. My line is a torpedo-head tapered number three, intended for dry-fly work, so I knew it would do very well, so long as the fish fed near the surface.

A fish rose beyond my reach but I cast in his direction. At about my sixth cast, I felt a touch which was not followed up at once. I waited a moment or two before sending the big lure on another trip to the same spot. This time it was taken with a jolt and a good rainbow raced away and leapt out of the water to flash in the air.

Rob wound in his line with a yell of delight to give me a clear run for my line, as the reel screamed like a siren. Here was certainly a fighting rainbow! Time and again I wound her in to the boat, and every time she took off once more with renewed vigour. At last, the strength left her and she was on her side by the boat. With a businesslike lift of the net which spoke of much practice Rob had her in the boat. Now I saw something new. My friend picked up a hammer and used it smartly to kill my fish. The young enthusiast then measured my trout with a steel tape at eighteen inches and recorded its weight at exactly three pouds.

The Parson's Glory might have expected that we would have used a proper priest to kill its capture instead of a common hammer, for it refused to catch another fish, and wound up slightly ruffled among the tiny dries in my hat where it now reposes, apparently quite at home.

Again, under my friend's skilled advice, I mounted my short-caster rod and a threadline reel. Rob handed me a thing I'd never seen before, which he called a yellow chicken. It was twice the size and several times the weight of the Parson's Glory, and its killing end was fitted with a sea hook. Under guidance I got the hang of how to cast with the hurling reel. To my utter surprise my chicken was grabbed by a rainbow of four pounds which measured twenty-one inches. Like the other one, it was a female and fought like a tiger. Again my friend flipped it into the net expertly and swung his hammer. I returned the deadly chicken to its owner. If I had stuck it in my hat the other flies would surely have taken off in terror.

The weather, uncertain all the time, now looked like breaking into a thoroughly unpleasant squall. As the waves rose higher and the boat bucked and rocked, we reeled up. It was sad to see Rob give up without having bent his rod.

The trolling runs he had planned, and for which he had fitted his Seagull outboard motor, were abandoned. We reached the shore only just in time to escape the squall and its attendant heavy rain.

So we loaded up and returned to Tokoroa. Rob was delighted with his guest's success, and the fact that he had enrolled a new member in the ranks of his very active Tokoroa Freshwater Angling Club.

24. *Waiteti Interlude*

The Waiteti Stream enters Lake Rotorua just north of Ngongotaha. Lovely as this place is, it does not convey any sign of trout water to anyone accustomed to the usual trout fishing streams of New Zealand.

At the mouth of the stream is an arched footbridge from which one looks upstream to see green lawns, shrubs bordering the stream to its edge. Large weeping willows here and there lend an old world charm to a peaceful scene of traditional residential life. For a chain or so above the footbridge a gravelled path abuts the edge of a private lawn. Here and there, short trampled paths lead to the water's edge. These, I was told, were made by anglers.

"You just cast across the stream towards the big willow in the evening, let your line sink, wait a minute or so and then start a slow retrieve," Mr Albert Aspden advised me.

This sounded like a leg-pull and incredible anyhow. Yet in this angling game no one can be too positive about anything. My doubts must have shown, and a sharp correction was in pickle.

At nine forty-five that night, I was reading Colonel Beamish's reference to New Zealand angling when a knock on the door of our motel unit startled me. It was Mr Albert Aspden of the motel.

"I thought," he said, "you might be interested to see a fish my brother, Cliff, has just caught at the footbridge."

There was Mr Cliff Aspden with a rod in one hand and a still kicking brown trout gripped by the gills in the other. The small red and brown fly was firmly embedded in the roof of the monster's mouth. I cut it out with my pen-knife and washed it under a tap to examine it. The hook was a size seven out-point with flat sides. The body was dark red mohair and the wing was probably a side-of-the-neck of bantam rooster. The tail was fur from a red squirrel.

The fish — we weighed it twice to make sure — was ten pounds and was in first-class condition.

"Tell me how you fished for it?" I asked.

"I just cast my fly out towards the willow and let it drift down. I took out a packet of cigarettes, lit one, put the packet back in my pocket, and then started to retrieve the line slowly. I'd only got it about half in when the fish took the fly."

"Have any trouble to land it?"

"No, Albert netted it in for me."

One cast, one cigarette, one fish!

And this on a spot I had judged the last place on earth one could get a fish of any kind.

Verily this angling is a mysterious business.

The next evening Cliff Aspden asked me to join him on the lake. We rowed about 300 yards off shore to find another boat was anchored on the exact spot we were headed for, so we had to put down our anchor quietly, a polite distance away.

As we moved into position we saw several good bulging rises and one fish leap clear of the water, so all appeared to be favourable.

Quite soon I got a touch on my Sierpinski and that was something. Cliff, who casts a long, well-laid line, also got a touch. That was to be our portion for that occasion.

Our neighbour, casting left handed with an easy grace that reflected long practice, suddenly spoke:

"Got one!"

"Good for you," we called.

It was not more than a pound and a half.

We carried on. I changed to a Black Dog; but Cliff — I doubt if he had a spare fly — stuck to his original.

Our neighbour spoke again: "Here's another!"

His rod bent to a better fish and his almost silent reel told of its effort to break away.

At last the fish was near the boat; we were shattered to see the angler lean over the side to grab at the fish by hand.

"Brother!" I called, "you can't do that!"

The fish smashed the water violently as the quiet voice spoke.

"A good way to lose a fish."

Cliff called, "Wait a tick; I'll pass you my landing net."

"It's all right," came the answer, as the three-pound rainbow was flopped into the boat.

"Are you from Malaysia?" Cliff asked, for some obscure reason.

"Why, no. I'm from California."

Cliff and I battled on.

"What fly did you bend on?" I was asked.

"A Hairy Dog that hasn't bitten anything yet."

The Californian hooked still another and there we watched as he played his fish almost to a standstill.

"I guess I'm in trouble now."

"What's wrong?"

"My line has snarled up."

That fish took advantage of the situation and broke free.

Again the voice addressed us. "I'm sorry to barther you gentlemen. Can you lend me a flashlight?"

We could not; and it looked to be the end for him as well. Though he was still working doggedly in the darkness over his snarled up line as we came away, bidding him good night.

"Good night." Then he added dismally. "We have to go home next week, Ah'm sorry to say. But Ah'm coming back; back to your wonderful country and your wonderful fishing."

There is interest in every kind of angling, even in this

harling business from an anchored boat. Yet once the dry fly has been adopted as the highest form of the art, there is always that hankering for it.

So I tried the upper reaches of the Ngongotaha Stream which has the reputation of being the best in the conservancy of Rotorua for this form of fishing.

Not knowing the water I just went to the reaches nearest the gate through which I had been directed; these reaches appeared to be rather shallow, but bright, sparkling and full of promise. I was able to wade wherever necessary in thigh waders as I worked upstream and, in the hour at my disposal, rose three fish; but all were undersized and returned carefully.

At a sharp bend I came across two wet-fly anglers, man and wife, who had just started. Their selected pool was deep and calm.

"Any encouragement?" I asked.

"No. It's early yet," the man answered. "When it's dark is the best time."

I watched their casting efforts which showed every fault imaginable.

"We're new chums at this game," the young man offered. "It's my first season."

"Oh well, we all had to start, you know," I said. "Don't get discouraged. You'll soon pick it up."

"Oh, we are all right," was the shattering reply. "I've caught thirty-five so far, mostly in this hole!"

I had asked for it. As I bade them "good evening", I'll swear I heard the young woman titter.

My last day saw me on the Kaituna River at the Trout Pool to which I had been taken by Stan Blackmore of Rotorua. It was a perfectly lovely evening for fishing, there being no wind to interfere with the casting.

To reach the Trout Pool we had to scramble down steep hillsides and round the end of a bank that hangs above the pool. We found ourselves on a small shelf just about the size of a kitchen sink bench. At our back the bank rose like a wall, overgrown with bracken fern and tutu bushes. These were a peril to the fly. Weeping willows to our left restricted casting room to about twenty feet. By casting high, we managed to avoid being hooked up.

The water swirled from our right in a strange action which I could not understand. Some currents changed direction and charged towards our shelf and the bank on our right. They then twisted along the bank again to volume under the willows on our left.

Rafts of creamy foam rode these currents, bearing witness to the tortured action the river had been through as it crashed over the great Okere Falls a mile or so upstream. Even before it reached the Trout Pool it had been churned up greatly in lesser falls of the rocky gorge. There was menace in the roar of the many waters.

Stan's calm voice said: "The pool seems to be in pretty good order. The spinners fall on the scum. The fish rise madly at these and the trick is to put your fly down on or near the foam patches."

As we waited for the hatch of flies to commence, we had sandwiches, hard-boiled eggs and hot tea which Mrs Blackmore had prepared for us. My friend entertained with anecdotes in which some of our angling pals had taken part, so time passed pleasantly until at last we saw the hatch. Up rose the duns in clouds and we watched the whirling of females above, and males rising from below. The cycle of events was fast, as male grasped female in mid-air to complete the sexual act for the perpetuation of the species.

Almost at once, it seemed, the female started her final upstream flight as she touched the water again and again on her egg-laying dance, while the males fell exhausted and helpless, as "spents", on the foamy water. This was the moment for the hungry trout, and they rose here, there and everywhere.

Stan, using a split-wing Kakahi Queen, plied his cast with skill. No fish accepted it.

We cast one at a time, there being so little room to work. My fly was hackle dressed with a tight quill body. It was nearly black; but so small it was difficult to see. I cast under direction and my friend, noted for his bluntness in fishing matters, accepted my efforts.

"Later they'll fall for it," Stan averred. "You'll see, about nine o'clock you'll see."

Nine o'clock! It was now nearly eight. We'd been on the sink-bench over three hours. How long can these fellows hang out? I wondered.

It must have been a disappointment to Stan that I had to give the game away. He quite cheerfully came with me still muttering invectives in strange words that a pool boiling with fish had completely baffled the two of us.

The dark, deep, swirling foamy river; the narrow ledge from which to cast; the claw-like bracken above and the innocent looking willows, which were more willing to take our flies than the rising fish, is one more memory of weird fishing experiences.

25. The Turbulent Tongariro

There are men who are born to catch fish. I have met them round the coasts and harbours of the North Island; I have met them on inland waters almost everywhere. There are just a few of them, and they seem to be able to get fish on their lines when the rest of us are just doing our best.

I was fishing the Tongariro with one of these rare people yesterday afternoon – in September 1966 – when fish were not taking notice, or were absent from home. My friend handed me his rod for a moment. I fished the cast out to its end without result, and handed the rod back. As soon as his hand closed on the handle a fish grabbed the fly. That the fish was a poor one is beside the point; what interested me was his remark: "That fish must have followed the fly all the way down and just took it at the bottom of its travel."

How did he know that the fish had followed the fly like that? Quite probably he was correct about what that fish had done, but I'm still wondering whether, if he had not taken the rod at that moment, *I* would have caught the trout.

Being more or less a new chum at the use of flies bigger than size eight, I was not confident on the large turbulent pools of the Tongariro with the big lures generally regarded as essential there.

For this reason I had spent much of my time watching my companion, Les Mark of Taumarunui.

It was really his idea that I should tackle the Tongariro river fishing. Acting on his advice I had purchased a nine foot fibreglass rod, a reel capable of carrying 130 yards of line, a wet-cell sinking line and heavy nylon casts, in order to be able to handle the mighty fighting rainbows of the famed river. It was also his idea that I should join him at the Water Tower that Tuesday morning.

All came to pass as planned and we met at ten a.m. Our first pool was the Red Hut, to approach which we had to cross the top of the reach on a flying fox, a professionally built and perfectly comfortable aerial gondola.

From this vehicle – it was twenty or thirty feet above the water – it was impressive to look down on the surging torrent. Here was power. Here was a place where a fisherman could use discretion or find himself in serious trouble.

Although there had been heavy rains the week before, the Taupo district had had four fairly fine days. In spite of this, the water was a bit cloudy – milky – and quite unsuitable for my little snobs, but "not bad" for my friend's Mallard and Yellow size four lure.

"No one here, Greg," he remarked, "but sometimes there are twenty rods here!"

There was a perfect dry-fly eye on the Red Hut Pool and I asked my friend to allow me to put a big Hairy Dog upon it from below. He stood back and waited as I worked out my line for the upstream cast. Of course, it was hopeless; the water wasn't clear enough and my line was a wet-cell (sinking) type. Although the fly dropped in the eye it was pulled below by the line at once. Disgusted at the poor effort, I let the line go down the current and swing round. The big black beast of a fly whacked itself into a rock and defied all my tricks to get it free. There the damn thing still remains.

After this lack of response I came up again and sat on a boulder to watch Les casting. It was pleasant sitting there in the sun. He entered the water well above the eye. Slowly and carefully he edged his way in until he was waist deep. His armpit waders still gave him several inches of freeboard. His great safety jacket made his upper structure look enormous. From this apparently awkward position he started casting. It was then the Little People, who play tricks on anglers, became active. Suddenly Les's Yellow and Mallard whipped off my hat and dropped it in the water. Only by bounding over the boulders did I manage to get to it in the nick of time and snatch it out, thus saving my little snobs from an ignominious end. What a sorry sight they looked all wet and bedraggled, completely shocked and outraged.

I shook as much as possible of the Tongariro off the hat and stuck it on a warm boulder where, in about an hour, the little snobs dried out and recovered much of their natural charm and good humour.

In the meantime I had sat down far enough back to keep out of trouble with the Little People and continued my studies of how to catch trout with a lure in the Tongariro River.

Les seemed to have no trouble getting his heavy line out across the water almost to the opposite bank. At once he stripped some yards more off the reel, and the quick water whipped the lot right down the river.

This is where I saw a new type of "fishing the fly". When the fly reached its limit of travel and started to swing in towards his own side of the stream, Les started to jiggle the fly in six-inch jerks letting it return to where it was and jerking it in the same way again. After half a dozen of these movements he then started an orthodox finger and thumb retrieve. Perhaps all wet-fly artists use this movement, but for those who do not know it I shall try to explain: the line is gripped between forefinger and thumb of the left hand below the butt-ring of the rod. The palm is upwards when the line is so gripped. Then the hand is rolled backwards toward the body, the fingers are spread so the little finger can engage the line at the spot below the butt-ring where the first grip was taken. This movement has the natural effect of pulling one's fly upstream five or six inches. As soon as the little finger is hooked on the line the hand is turned back again to the upturned position. This pulls the fly a further five or six inches upstream.

As far as I understand this trick, it represents the short jerky movement of some bug, beetle, crayfish, creeper, tadpole or other form of sub-aquatic life doing something down there; and the fish, from a desire to catch it, eat it, or just to be aggressive, grabs the thing and gets caught on the hook.

It has been my experience that this retrieving movement is carried on until the line that was cast is shortened to a convenient length for recasting. It is coiled in the natural figure-of-eights in the palm of the left hand where it is loosely retained by the fingers of the left hand.

This was not the way Les Mark was doing it. If after five, six or perhaps seven hand rolls there was no "take" by a fish, he gave it up, and reaching his left hand up to the butt-ring, stripped the whole of his casting line back into his left hand in rapid six-foot long loops. As soon as he had as much back as suited his purpose, out went the line again on a fresh journey down the pool. Each cast was made after he had moved down the current cautiously for a yard or two, so new water was being fished each time.

In this system the angler obviously thinks it is a waste of time to patiently recoil the line in the over-hand — or rolling hand — the whole way up again. The "hot-spot" at the bottom of the fly's movement is that few feet of first upstream jiggle and crawl.

I had fished with Les Mark many times before on lakes and smaller streams and had never seen him do this. It is quite clear that for Tongariro pools and such, or hard water, the style he was using that day is a tremendous saver of time.

Les said he was sorry that he had got me down there on a day when the trout were "off", but he need not have worried. My wife and I had a most enjoyable day and for me, as well, an enlightening one.

Desiring, I suppose, to show us that things were not always

so dull, he produced his angling diary. This showed that
from May 7 to August 28 he had, in seven days, taken
eighty-nine rainbow trout—eighty-one from the Tongariro
River and eight (the limit) from Lake Rotoaira. I quote
from his record: "25th July on Tong. 4 fish from the Hut
[this is not the Red Hut]. Lot of snags there [did he mean
sticks or fishermen?], foul-hooked 1 in Island pool, took 9
from Red Hut, came on for an hour, Orange & Mallard
went very well. Bath over full with 14." The bath is a pink
one of plastic made for mothers to wash babies.

Another entry: "7th May Tongariro. A good fish off the
Pulpit took 25 minutes to land, 6 lbs. Another from Island
pool 4 lbs. Went back Pulpit, above this time, water high,
fish under banks, several good pulls, then a good fish 7 or
8 lbs, after 10 minutes lost him as Mr & Mrs G. came over.
Again up to Pulpit, lost one; struck heavy pull, long fight
just a steady down-boring to bottom. After 35 mins decided
to force it downstream or would never land it, so waded
straight in and down the middle of the river to land it in 3
inches of water at the Island Pool. An enormous brown jack
with big up-turned bottom jaw. 11 lbs. Took 45 minutes to
land. S. suggested that it be entered for the annual competi-
tion [the Whitney Cup] for the heaviest fish caught in Taupo
for the season. So up to the club house — The Tongariro and
Lake Taupo Anglers' Club, Turangi — so the Admiral and
others could see it."

I saw this big fish when I called at Mr Mark's home on my
way home from my duck shooting at Ohura. It was then
hard frozen in his deep freezer. Five-pound and six-pound
trout in near-by containers looked small in comparison.

26. Night Fishing

In places like Taupo and Rotorua it is possible that more fish are caught at night than during the day. Apart from the fact that more people are able to go fishing at night, there is the more important fact that fish are easier to catch at sundown and afterwards.

Favourite places are where a stream, even a small one, enters the lake, or off a point jutting into the lake. This holds true for all times, but particularly in the darkening hours. Trout food appears to be more easily found inshore and the fish feel safer close in at night.

Experts tell us brownies are very hard to catch in the daytime, and they recommend special flies and methods to take them at night. For the life of me I cannot see why these should be considered necessary.

Nor do I quite agree that brown trout are "very hard" to catch in the daytime. If this were true, the South Islanders, whose rivers are stocked with little or nothing else, would have a pretty thin time; instead of which they enjoy wonderful fishing as well as most delightful conditions.

I have never been very happy fishing at night because of a frightening ordeal I experienced when I was nine. This occurred on the Lerdiderg River in Victoria. I had discovered a "hole" above an irrigation weir where the fishing was excitingly good. There on other nights I had caught blackfish, gudgeon and eels. To get to this place it was necessary to edge my way round a perpendicularly cut bank above the very deep hole to fish from a narrow sloping ledge. Off this ledge the water went straight down. On the bank above a big messmate gumtree stood. The messmate, being a deep rooter, had big roots sticking out of the cut bank which had been eroded away from them.

My only light was one of my uncle's carriage lamps, a square-headed thing which held a candle in the stem. It was the work of a moment to dig a hole in the clay bank, a foot or so above the water, in which to stick the stem of the lamp. The ideal was to have the light shine on my cork floater which, by the way, I still have. All went according to plan.

By this time I was a pretty successful fisher, so it was not long before I was excitedly dealing with fish. Several black-fish and an eel or two were in the bag before I started to fish for the gudgeon. To get these black and yellow cod-shaped fellows I used smaller hooks and dipped the bait, a worm, in oil of rhodium, supposed to make the bait irresistible.

In the middle of these operations I was startled to hear the lamp splutter; the next minute it went out. I realised the river was rising and I was trapped on the ledge.

As quickly as I could I rammed the lamp in on top of my fish, lashing the lot to the reel end of my rod. I then tried to get off the ledge the way I had entered. I began to edge my way through the swirling water which was nearly knee deep, but gave that up.

My one chance, a slim one, was to climb up the cut bank by the projecting roots of the tree. Luckily I was a skinny kid and blessed with strong fingers. I had to feel for a root and grip it hard, tugging a bit to test it. If it held I'd kick a toe-hold into the bank and then grope for another root higher up. Some were rotten and gave way, but there was always one sound enough. At long last my fingers closed on a smooth, snake-like root that ran straight up and down. This was the tap root of an old lucerne plant, for we were in lucerne country, and at that moment I knew I was safe. Each hand grip on the rope-like root had to be dug out with the fingers, but this was not so bad, as the soil was softer up there. When

K

I was able to reach out my hand on the top to grab a lucerne head, it was a matter of a moment to drag myself up over the edge to level ground.

When I got my wind and reached down to get my rod I just managed to take hold of the tip. I dragged the lot up, the bag and all in it a sopping mess. The eels were still writhing, but I knew they were dead all right.

I saw the river next morning when my aunt sent me with a message to Broadacres station. From the road bridge below the weir a raging yellow flood greeted me: a hypo to fix the picture of the night before so that it's with me still.

That experience taught me to take care of myself, but it left me with a built-in aversion to fishing at night by myself. For all that I enjoy a bit of shadow sparring in agreeable company. I remember a grand night's fun about 1954 when, as their guest, I fished with four rangers of the Wildlife Branch of the Internal Affairs Department during a week's refresher course in Turangi. Our working days had been long and pretty tough, so when it came to the second last evening, our leader, my old friend Major Frank Yerex, then Wildlife controller, declared a night off.

"I suggest, gentlemen," he said in his best manner, "we devote tonight to some practical experience of Taupo angling. Anyone short of gear, let me know, and he will be fixed up."

As far as I was concerned I had to borrow everything. The flies in my own hat were so small that the trout of the lake would have needed spectacles to see them.

My cabin mate, Foster Hamlett of Rotorua, led us first to the outlet of the Waiotaka River. The water looked pretty rough when we started and got worse and worse. It was not long before I was a mere looker-on from the beach. "Blast this place," someone growled out of the dark. "Let's go and have a swim in the spa baths at Tokaanu, then go on to fish at Slip Creek. It'll be sheltered there from this wind."

As we came away we met two young Maoris with their rods on the way in. Someone else spoke to them, charitably informing them of the bad conditions at the lake and the absence of fish. "Oh, well," one of them drawled. "We taihoa (wait) a bit, she might come orright."

We tore off to the baths and had a by no means silent dip in the thermal water. Soon we were in waders again and ready for action where this small stream enters the lake at no great distance from the historic village of Waihi. It is here that the great Chief Heu Heu, who granted as a free gift the Tongariro National Park to the people of New Zealand, lies at rest.

Foster placed me on his left; the others spaced themselves out on his right. One of these got a fish almost at once. Foster took one about half an hour later and I went ashore to see him land it. When he got it out on the beach we saw it was a slab. I told him a friend of mine in Taumarunui would advise him to use that fish as a bookmark. He took the joke in good part. In a short time he had another fish on. This was a better one. My industrious casting and retrieving had been of no avail. Foster wound in. "Here, take my fly and I'll take yours."

A few minutes after this I hooked one. It put up a poor fight and I wasn't surprised to see another bookmark. My next fish would not have won a beauty contest either. I lost another which seemed to have a bit of character and which might have saved mine, but, as I say, he was lost. And for me, that was all.

As far as I can remember no one caught a fish in the last hour. Foster called: "Time, gentlemen, please. Time, gentlemen, please." It was eleven o'clock and it seemed we were all glad.

Five men, five hours, seven fish, the very best of which could be called only fair.

As I rolled up my line, I glanced up at the stars. They were glowing brilliantly. A skein of swans flew heavily over our heads calling their cracked, scratchy notes to the lovely night.

"Where are they going? I've never seen swans on Taupo."

"Motuopa Bay. They have a beat there somewhere," came the answer.

We learned next morning that our hearts need not have bled for the two poor Maori boys we had met at the Waiotaka.

As a reward for their "taihoa", the lake had "come orright" and they had taken twelve beautiful fish! A glance at the map of Lake Taupo shows the bird-line from Waihi to the Waiotaka outlet is only about four miles. Why, during the same hours on the same night, fish were poor in the one and good in the other is a mystery.

My knowledge of lure fishing at Taupo has been enlarged through the friendly coaching of John Sierpinski who has taken me to some of his favourite spots around the lake such as Kinloch, Whakaipo Bay, Waipehi (Jellicoe Point), Hatepe, Waitahanui "up-river only" and quite a few others. Through him I have had a fair measure of success and some very good sport. He also straightened out a number of my wrong views about night fishing, not by words but by actual demonstration.

When fishing at night, John replaces his Ugly Duckling with a Pukeko. This is not remarkable, as trout see black things against the sky better than light ones. What did interest me was to see him greasing a floating line, or rather, changing his wet-fly reel for one that had a dry-fly line on it, and fishing it downstream with a wet fly. It looked all wrong, especially when his gut cast was only two feet in length.

The use of a greased line downstream was fully explained in Anthony Crossley's book on salmon and sea-trout fishing published by Methuen in 1939.

I tried Crossley's method twenty years ago in both the Whakapapa and Wanganui rivers without conspicuous success, concluding that it was useful for salmon and sea-trout only. Now I saw an experienced angler using it for rainbow at night. In mid-August, about four o'clock, we left for Kinloch, an attractive bay on the western side of the lake. There is a clean little rivulet running busily into the lake across a gently shelving beach where John said he had fished before. At first we used sinking lines and Ugly Ducklings without moving anything. By now it was dusk so we decided to rest the water while we had our snack of sandwiches and hot tea. We sat on a grassy bank near a faintly rustling flax bush, watching the opalescent glow of Taupo town spread on the clouded sky and lights spring out along the shores of the far side of the lake.

"Come, we catch a fish," John declared. "We change to floating lines and put on the Pukeko."

The fish, however, didn't seem to care much what we did. Then John got a fish on and lost it; almost at the same time I did the same with the same result. At seven-twenty a fish of three pounds two ounces fixed himself firmly to my Pukeko. He fought rather poorly, I thought, but in fact he was by no means a bad little fellow.

Shortly afterwards the weather became cold and squally and we went home.

I again joined John on August 29 at the same place but in better weather. This was to be my most successful night. Again the floating line and the Pukeko fly on a short cast method was adopted. I landed two fine rainbows: female, four pounds six ounces; male, three pounds five ounces. Both were in first-class condition. I came away at eight-thirty leaving my friend the sole occupant of the beach; but on this occasion he did not increase his score – to date – of 193.

There is still only one river in which I can fish at night without feeling nervous. It's a stream I "married" many years ago. I have camped in a tent within yards of it on many a holiday. Its pools became so familiar to me that I seemed to know every bush and boulder. Many, many of its splendid fish have risen to my floating fly or darted on my nymph, and scores have thrown my hook or broken my cast. Plenty of times my dear river has tipped me upside down and her icy biting water goosefleshed my hide; but this was just the scolding of a well-wishing friend. I do not need to mention the charmer's name.

27. A Word and its Meaning

Within my first month in New Zealand I met a puzzling word. It came from the lips of an English visitor to Canterbury who was fishing the Waimakariri River. I was to remember the word which stood for something that was to become a lifetime interest to me: acclimatisation.

The angler was knee deep in a clear galloping reach, casting his fly upstream. I waded across a couple of small rills in order to get a closer look. He called, "You are wet!"

"Yes, it's rather fun. I've never been able to do this before."

"Where on earth do you come from?"

"From a dried-up part of Victoria, Australia," I answered.

"What are you fishing for?"

"Trout, of course."

The Oxford accent was unmistakable. He couldn't be English, I thought, or he would not have spoken to me. But he was. The difference? He was an angler.

"Are trout natural here?"

"No. They are salmo fario from England. Brown trout, y'know."

"Who brought them here?"

"Who took them to Australia?" he countered.

"A parson," I said. "The reverend Mr Yeo."

He roared with laughter. "Bay Jove, old chap, you have a sense of humour. I'll bet a penny that a parson brought them to this colony."

He waded over to me. "Rarely, you must let me carry you back to dray land."

"I'm eleven stone," I said, deciding it would be great fun to be borne across the current on the back of an English gentleman. He staggered a bit but got me to dry land.

"I'd like to taste this trout fishing. I could not catch them in Victoria."

"What did you use?"

"Worms."

"Good God!" he cried out. "Surely not."

I could see my stocks going down. "Oh," I said, "I have tried a painted minnow, but that was no good."

"Rarely, old chap, you must only use flays for trout. Worms and so on are only for coarse fishing. If you get a licence I'll teach you to use a flay, if you wish."

"Who issues a licence?" This was a new idea to me.

"The Acclimatisation Society, y'know. It only costs a sovereign."

What the hell was an acclimatisation society? I thought.

"Thank you very much. I'm afraid that fishing is out of my reach just yet. I hope you catch a trout."

"Dear me! Only . . . Oh, I hope so, old chap, I hope so." As I climbed the bank, he called:

"I say, old chap, what sort of fish did you catch in Australia?"

"Native trout, perch, gudgeon, blackfish . . ."

"Blackfish. What are they like? We have gudgeon and perch in England and many other coarse fish, but tell me about blackfish."

I told him they were similar to perch, but black all over, very black, growing to about two pounds, as far as I knew, but my biggest was a bit over a pound. Good eating, with a lot of bones. That was about all I could tell him, except they were our favourite fish.

With that I bade him good-bye, and he let me go.

In after years, when I took up fishing, this stranger's words influenced my way with a rod. For his gentlemanly treatment of an inquisitive intruder, his kindly solicitude about my getting wet, his offer to give up his fishing time to teach an unknown youth, I have always been grateful. "If you get a licence" – the first thing he thought of. "You must always use flies for trout." "I'll teach you to use a fly, if you wish." In these things I have tried to follow his principles.

When I got back to the farm where I was working on a clover shelling machine, I asked Tom Hodgens, the manager, about this acclimatisation business and learned that these societies were composed of rod and gun sportsmen actively engaged in the sport; and naturalists, who were all interested in providing game and fish for their licence holders who made up the total membership. Their only revenue came from licence money. Mr Hodgens also said that rangers were employed by the society and had the powers of a policeman under the Fish and Game Acts. Protection of native birds was included in the work.

"Why the jawbreaking name, Tom?"

"Introduced things have to get used to the climate of their new home. A lot of things can't, and fail. We just have to put up with the jaw breaker." We still do.

My interest in acclimatisation matters started with the sport of shooting, particularly deerstalking, ten years after my first angling lecture when I made friends of the two stipendiary rangers for the Wellington Society, Percy Willson and Clarrie Bould, and came to appreciate the tough conditions under which they worked and the devotion they had for the wild things under their care, particularly the vanishing native birds. Through them I met the secretary, Mr C. I. Dasent, from whom I gained a greater share of information about acclimatisation matters. I was to be made aware, for instance, that thousands of anglers throughout the Dominion spent a lot of time and money to establish trout and salmon in the waters under their control. How much we owe to these men, whose work made New Zealand one of the best trout-fishing countries in the world, can hardly be estimated. Under their advice and guidance, legislators have written a code of laws that are so reasonable that any man worth his salt should be proud to obey. My unknown angler from England sixty years ago was plainly one of these. The thought of unfair lures, like worms, was abhorrent to him. And so, too, it is with many thousands of our fellows. The laws allow for the purist as well as for him who likes to get his trout on a hardware bait. There are the fish for both. Beautiful fish.

Trout liberations were, and are, not all made in easily reached waters. Sometimes mountain streams run in remote places, and, in earlier days, were extremely difficult to reach with trout fry. The Waimarino Society controls many such streams in the Central King Country south of Taumarunui. Recently I called on Mr Tom Shout at Raetihi who was president of that body for a great part of its lifetime and asked him to tell me fully the story of one of the ten annual liberations which he and Mr A. C. Henderson, their secretary for well over fifty years, made in the early days, 1920–30.

Mr Shout told me that about 1920 Mr John Cullen of the National Park Board had requested, on behalf of the board, rainbow fry for liberation in Lake Tama and the upper streams of Ruapehu Mountain including both branches of the Whakapapa River. Mr Cullen had a hut on the Tawhai near the latter stream (actually Whakapapaiti) which he allowed the officers of the society to use.

"I usually left the Rotorua hatcheries with about fifty thousand fry in cans," Mr Shout said, "and travelled with the fry in the guard's van all the way to Waimarino station (now National Park station). Of course the water had to be changed where possible and kept agitated as much as could be done, one way or the other.

"I would leave Rotorua at six-twenty in the morning for Frankton Junction, and change trains for Taumarunui. Again a new train had to be built there which finally got us to Waimarino station at midnight. There we were met by Dick Cliff, with a dray, and Alex (Henderson). The dray got us to Cullen's camp. When we got there we submerged the cans in the Tawhai Stream. And for the next two or three days we'd be distributing the fry in different streams.

"On one September afternoon we were on the way with some fry for the smaller of the two Tama lakes, (4,240 feet) when we ran into a southerly blizzard. This got so bad that the horses refused to go any further; and there we were. Alex said: 'There is only one thing to do now, Tom.' Of course I thought he meant we should go back. But that was not his idea at all.

"'We'll have to carry the cans ourselves.' And that's just what we did. We tied the horses up in a sheltered spot and went on with the cans. We'd pick the horses up on the way home.

"On one of the streams we had to cross on the way back, Alex said there was a ford. By this time it was dark. I went down and then called back, 'There's no ford here, Alex. I'm up to my knees and it's getting deeper all the time.'

"'Oh,' Alex said, 'give the horse his head.'

"I did this and the horse turned around and went a few chains upstream, and there was the ford. The horse knew.

"When we got back to the camp about ten o'clock, Alex made one of his rare long speeches, 'Tom. This has been the coldest day I have ever felt in my life.' And that, for a Clutha man, was something."

Plainly those two men were acclimatised.

28. The Whakapapa

On a recent summer evening I followed a well-known track from Te Whare Ra down to the Whakapapa River. The track zig-zags left and right through manuka and odd splashes of purple broom as it descends the steep bank down to the old stile of a broken-down fence that once divided the pasture land above from the swamp that runs parallel to the river. Old planks and boards form a precarious duck-walk across the marshy parts. Here, too, the track is just wide enough for the angler to get through the scrub and raupo leaves without getting hooked up in the vines and overhanging tree-tops. This passage is kept open by anglers by the constant use of bush knife and fern-hook. In a single season of neglect it can close up completely under the lush growth of swamp vegetation.

It was here one afternoon that two fern-birds (*Bowdleria punctata*) responded to my calling of fantails which I was doing to amuse my wife. Suddenly, she saw what at first she thought were two rats, and registered suitable gasps of fear; but then was thrilled when I told her she was being honoured, by fern-birds. They crept furtively through the leaves of raupo and were not afraid to come within a yard or two. Truda noticed their long raggy tails and I was able to tell her that the bird uses his tail when climbing up a stem of raupo – they never seem to live in fern at all – looking for insects. Naturally, these tail feathers get a bit raggy.

In this small swamp I have heard the purring note of a spotless crake, but never saw the maker, and did not know for some years what bird had made it.

Another bird-note heard there several times about 1946 was never identified. It was a clear bell call of five bars that rose boldly up and down. Dr Falla, the ornithologist, thought it might have been the call of a North Island thrush, but being unable to get up to my cottage did not hear it himself. Although heard over several months that year it was never heard afterwards. Swamps are always mysterious places.

I sat down on a large boulder between the water and the lupin bushes that line the bank, and watched over what had been left by the floods of my beloved Apron Pool. There was nothing new about this. I had sat on many boulders and logs along the Whakapapa for over thirty years watching and waiting for a fish to rise. On this evening there was no sign of a fish and few insects were to be seen.

A friendly voice broke into my thoughts: "What are you doing sitting there, Greg? Contemplating nature?"

"I'm not contemplating nature, you mug," I answered rudely. "I'm waiting for a rise."

My friend, Peter McIntyre, who now has a cottage and studio on the high bank above, had brought his rod down to join me for the evening's fishing.

"Well, let's get going," he remarked mildly. "The water is not quite clear."

After all, Peter was correct. Angling and contemplation of nature are inseparable. Both demand calm and peace. As angling calls for keen observation of events and changes in weather, light, and water, so does success or failure with the rod call for experience and wisdom and philosophic acceptance. If contemplation allows us time to winnow the golden grains of happiness from the tares and vetches of less attractive things, then surely Peter was right. I had indeed been contemplating nature in retrospect on the banks of my cherished river, the Whakapapa.

P. 158

Ugly Duckling Fly. P.117.

  Size 5 Limerick Turned Down Eye
  Alternate Bands of Black & Red Darning Wool

  B R B R

First Black 3 Strands upright ¼"
Then of Red
Then Wasps Black Fuzzy fur from the
Tail of Oppossum taken in sparingly
& left protruding at the tail.

Dipping bait (worm) in oil of rhodium
makes it irresistible.